Stimulating Story Writin

Inspiring children aged 7–11

Simon Brownhill

Contributions by Emma Hughes-Evans

Routledge
Taylor & Francis Group

LONDON AND NEW YORK

First published 2016
by Routledge
2 Park Square, Milton Park, Abingdon, Oxon OX14 4RN

and by Routledge
711 Third Avenue, New York, NY 10017

Routledge is an imprint of the Taylor & Francis Group, an informa business

© 2016 Simon Brownhill

British Library Cataloguing in Publication Data
A catalogue record for this book is available from the British Library

Library of Congress Cataloging in Publication Data
Brownhill, Simon, author.
Stimulating story writing! : inspiring children aged 7-11 / Simon
Brownhill ; contributions by Emma Hughes-Evans.
pages cm
Includes bibliographical references and index.
1. Creative writing (Elementary education)--Great Britain. 2. English language--Composition and exercises--Study and teaching (Elementary)--Great Britain. I. Title.
LB1576.B784 2016
372.62'3--dc23
2015016525

ISBN: 978-1-138-80482-1 (hbk)
ISBN: 978-1-138-80483-8 (pbk)
ISBN: 978-1-315-75269-3 (ebk)

Typeset in Sabon
by Saxon Graphics Ltd, Derby

To 'Simon's Group' – past, present and future

Contents

Acknowledgements

It is with the most heartfelt thanks that the following people are recognised:

- To Emma for all of her incredible hard work in editing each of the Ideas which made up the first 'messy' draft of this book, enriching them all with her numerous contributions – *thank you, thank you, thank you!*
- To my amazing family – Mom and Pop, Sugarfluff and Bro, Geoff and Eve, and Wilf the dog – thank you for your continued love and support.
- To the Fishers – I am very lucky to know and have you in my life.
- To all of my friends, both established, online and new – thanks for being my bud.
- To my godson, Curtis Jnr – I cannot tell you how proud I am to have been asked to be a part of your life.
- To the many wonderful colleagues I work with at the University of Cambridge, many of whom I consider to be my friend – thank you for your support.
- To all of the interpreters, co-trainers, administration, senior management and many trainers I have had the good fortune of working with on the CoE programme in Kazakhstan.
- All at Routledge, especially Annamarie and Sarah, for their diligent efforts in putting me in print once again.

Thank you all very much indeed.

SPB

Glossary and abbreviations

The following terms/abbreviations are used consistently throughout this professional book:

aka	also known as
BBC	British Broadcasting Corporation
BEd	Bachelor of Education
BFI	British Film Institute
C&C	Continue and Complete
CD	Compact disc
Child author	Any young person who mark makes/writes stories
CPD	Continuing Professional Development
DfE	Department for Education
DfES	Department for Education and Schools
DJ	Disc jockey
DVD	Digital versatile disc
EYFS	Early Years Foundation Stage (3–5+ years old)
GPS	Global positioning system
ICT	Information and Communication Technology
IPD	Initial Professional Development
IWB	Interactive whiteboard
KS1	Key stage 1 (5–7 years old)
KS2	Key stage 2 (7–11 years)
LKS2	Lower Key stage 2 (7–9 years old)
MPS	Medical Protection Society
n.d.	No date of publication indicated
NASA	National Aeronautics and Space Administration (USA)
NBC	National Broadcasting Company (American commercial broadcast television and radio network)
NHS	National Health Service
NICE	National Institute of Health and Clinical Excellence
OECD	Organisation for Economic Co-operation and Development
OFSTED	Office for Standards in Education, Children's Services and Skills
ONS	Office for National Statistics
Oracy	Speaking and listening
OUP	Oxford University Press

PGCE	Postgraduate Certificate in Education
PHSCE	Personal, Health, Social and Citizenship Education
PISA	Programme for International Student Assessment
POV	Point of view
Professional	Anyone who supports child authors in their learning, be they a volunteer, training (student), or qualified (teacher, teaching assistant)
R&B	Rhythm and blues
SCITT	School-Centred Initial Teacher Training
SEND	Special Educational Needs and Disabilities
SOAR	Situations, Obstacles, Actions, Results
Story	An account of imaginary or real people/beings and events told to inform, educate and entertain; synonyms include *narrative*, *tale*, *yarn*, *fable*, *fiction*
TRUCE	Teachers Resisting Unhealthy Children's Entertainment
UK	United Kingdom
UKS2	Upper Key stage 2 (9–11 years old)
USA	United States of America
VCOP	Verbs, Connectives, Openers, Punctuation
VIP	Very important person
WOW words	Adventurous and exciting language choices
Writing	The representation of language in a textual medium through the use of a set of signs or symbols that have meaning for the writer (child author)

Key stage bandings

The following Key stage bandings are used in this professional book to indicate particular age groups that different ideas are recommended for:

Key stage banding	Abbreviation	Alternative reference	Age group
Lower Key stage 2	LKS2	Lower Juniors	7–9
Upper Key stage 2	UKS2	Upper Juniors	9–11

Professionals are kindly reminded that the Key stage bandings offered in this professional book are *merely a recommendation*; readers may wish to select and use ideas offered in Key stage bandings that are different to the one they train/work in to positively respond to the needs and abilities of the child authors that they have the good fortune of working with.

Introduction

Six small cards were shuffled and carefully dealt, face down, in a row on the table.

Go on – pick one!

The man looked at the cards for a moment, reached out and selected one, turning it over in his hand. On the card was written a question: What?

The man thought for a moment and then began to type...

What is this book all about?

This book, as its title so aptly describes, is all about stimulating story writing – 'stimulating' in the sense of arousing children's interest and enthusiasm *for* story writing and 'stimulating' in the sense of ensuring that the stories children write are interesting *in content*, both for those who write them and those who read them. It focuses its attention on helping professionals to continue to 'reinvigorate' (OFSTED, 2009: 25) story writing provision in their respective classrooms/schools. A detailed exploration of the two dimensions which make up the Programmes of Study for Writing at KS2 – 'transcription (spelling and handwriting) [and] composition (articulating ideas and structuring them in speech and writing)' (DfE, 2013: 5) – largely fall out of the remit of this book; while the importance of these cannot be underestimated, professionals are encouraged to seek other sources for support (be they academic or professional) if their interest lies more in aspects such as writing development, handwriting or grammatical terminology. What is *central* to this book, however, is the interrelatedness of *spoken language*, *reading* and *writing* in KS2 (see DfE, 2013: 3) which implicitly underpin the thinking and ideas that are presented in this book.

Readers will note that links to the *English Programmes of Study: Key stages 1 and 2 – National Curriculum in England* (DfE, 2013) are *implicit* in the body of this book as opposed to them being explicit in nature; a conscious decision was made to ensure that all available wordage for the writing of this book could be channelled into providing professionals with an abundance of ways to stimulate children's story writing as opposed to 'tying' every idea and suggestion to statutory and non-statutory curriculum requirements.

Quite simply, this book has been written to offer those who work with children in educational contexts with a bounty of story writing ideas, practical learning and teaching strategies, academic information and thinking, research-informed guidance, *Gold star!* suggestions, and 'tried-and-tested' resources and activities to complement, energise and enrich professionals' evolving/established story writing provision and practice. It is strongly believed that committed professionals should actively seek a multitude of ways to engage children in exciting and purposeful story writing activity as part of a balanced curriculum: this is what this book aims to provide.

The man stopped typing, stretched, and looked over at the five remaining cards on the table.

Go on – pick another!

The man selected a second card – on this one was written a different question: Why?

The man's fingers approached the keyboard...

Why has this book been written?

There are numerous reasons as to why this book has been written; these are offered in bullet point form below and are merely presented in the order in which they came to mind:

- to satisfy the author's personal desire to write;
- to help and support professionals who work with children in educational contexts with regard to story writing;
- to energise story writing provision and practices in schools with regard to planning, resources, learning and teaching strategies and creative story writing ideas;
- to put the 'theory-into-practice' and the 'practice-into-theory' by making readers aware of academic thinking and research to support and strengthen professional practices associated with the teaching of story writing; and
- to purposefully engage children in rich and stimulating story writing activity.

This book has been written amidst the publication of various statistics that have recently appeared in national reports and international study findings linked to 'standards' in schools and the 'achievements' of children and young people. In 2013 the OECD reported that the PISA 2012 results for the UK showed 'no change in performance' in English (p. 1) when compared with the results from PISA 2006 and PISA 2009. From a national perspective, in 2012 the DfE stated that '[w]riting is the subject with the worst performance compared with reading, maths and science at Key stages 1 and 2' (p. 3). Reported statistics highlight that:

- 14 per cent of children at the end of KS1 in 2014 failed to meet the expected standard in writing (OFSTED, 2014);
- 21 per cent of children at the end of KS2 failed to meet level 4 or above in all of reading, writing and mathematics combined (DfE, 2014).

It is important to stress that this book makes *no* claim in being able to directly address and rapidly reduce these concerning percentages. What it does aim to do, however, is offer professionals ways to provide children with exciting opportunities to 'writ[e stories] for enjoyment' (OFSTED, 2009: 50) and 'engage and motivate pupils through practical, creative and purposeful [writing] activities' (p. 53). By doing this it is hoped that children will be more motivated to *want* to write and, with focused taught input and practice, they will be able to write *well*, which in turn will positively impact on both formative and summative assessment results. Readers are therefore encouraged to be mindful that the success or 'impact' of this book is *not* to be measured on the number of children who achieve or exceed governmental floor targets or 'standards' in their classroom/school – it is more about *stimulating* children and instilling in them a *passion* for putting pen to paper/finger to keyboard and writing stories (see Hodgins, 2001).

After answering his phone the man returned to the laptop.

This time why not pick *two* cards!

The man immediately chose two cards that were next to each other. On one it read: Where?; *on the other it read:* When?

Tap-tap-tap *went the keys on the man's laptop...*

Where and when can this book be used?

There are many setting and school types that the ideas in this book can be used in, a selection of which is offered below:

Primary schools	Junior schools	First schools	Middle schools
Academies	Hospital schools	Prep schools	Free schools
After-school clubs	Faith schools	Childminders	Special schools
Holiday clubs/sessional provision		Private/Independent schools	

In light of the above, it is worth acknowledging the different professionals that this book has been written to support (the *Who this book is written for*); the table below is adapted from Brownhill (2013: 5) in an effort to summarise a selection of the wide readership that this professional book aims to serve:

Those who are training or volunteering	• Practice-based qualifications at Level 2 and Level 3 • Initial Teacher Training e.g. BEd, PGCE, SCITT, School Direct • Education-based degrees e.g. Foundation, Child and Youth, Education Studies • Volunteers e.g. parent/carer helpers
Those in the infancy of their career	• Recently awarded professionals with Level 2 and Level 3 practice-based qualifications • Newly qualified teachers e.g. Junior, Primary
Those who are established in their working role	• Class teachers e.g. Junior, Primary, SEND, supply • Teaching assistants/learning support/mentors/HLTAs • Co-ordinators e.g. English, Literacy • Senior management members e.g. head teachers, deputy head teachers, assistant head teachers, school governors • Lecturers e.g. college (FE) and university (HE)

The professionals identified on the previous page (and others) are encouraged to use this book in a variety of different ways to support both their initial/continuing professional development (IPD/CPD) and their provision and practice in the classroom/school. A selection of possible ideas is provided in the grid below:

Learning and teaching strategies can be integrated into existing literacy planning (daily, weekly, medium term)	Suggested resources (writing/practical stimuli) can be collected, made or purchased for particular year groups	Academic and professional readings from the book can be read and discussed as part of a 'professional conversation' during a team/staff meeting
Story ideas can be used to stimulate child authors' homework/summer work activity	Ideas and information from the book can be used to inform action research projects currently being undertaken by professionals	Ideas can be used to support coaching and mentoring activity within the school; they can also be used to contribute to lesson study preparations
Network clusters can discuss, adapt and review the effectiveness of suggested ideas in this book with fellow professionals	Activities, ideas and suggestions can be shared with parents and carers during Open Days or Parent/Carer Writing Workshops	Academic and professional readings can be read and used to support the writing of coursework assignments as part of one's professional studies

There are just two cards left – pick one!

The man selected one of the cards and looked at it: Who?

'Well, I've already answered that!' *thought the man. There was thus only one card left.*

'I bet it says "How?"' *thought the man. He guessed correctly.*

How is this book organised and how can it be used?

A scan of the contents pages (pp. vii–x) indicates that this book is made up of ten chapters, each one containing nine main Ideas linked to the chapter focus and a 'Story writing "pick and mix"' to close the chapter with. The book is organised into two main parts. Part I is made up of Chapters 1 to 6, each one of which focuses its attention on a different story element; these are presented in the grid below:

Chapter number	1	2	3	4	5	6
Chapter title	Creating characters!	Super settings!	The plot thickens!	Colourful conflict!	Resolving the problem/s!	All's well that ends well!
Associated story element	Character	Setting	Plot	Conflict	Resolution	Ending

Part II is made up of the four remaining chapters, each one exploring different ways to stimulate story writing, namely through the use of inspired ideas (Chapter 7), resources (Chapter 8) and open-ended stimuli (Chapter 9). The final chapter (Chapter 10) addresses the 'great difficulty [of actually] getting started' (Selznick, 2012: 115) by offering professionals an array of practical and effective ways to help child authors put pen to paper/finger to keyboard and actually write stimulating stories!

Each Idea initially gives a brief explanation of the main focus and then offers suggestions that can be used and adapted for child authors across the full 7–11 age range. A *Gold star!* submission is offered at the end of each Idea to further invigorate story writing provision, practice and understanding; many of these are not directly connected to the main Idea described but they do serve as an integral feature to stimulating story writing as a whole.

Readers can engage with this book in a number of different ways:

- a *pick and mix* approach in which ideas and suggestions are randomly selected for use;
- a *cover-to-cover* approach which allows the reader to fully understand and embrace the book as a whole;
- an *element* approach which allows professionals to focus their attention on a specific story element (chapter) that they are teaching or on an area of need for their child authors; or
- a *zone-in* approach where readers use the contents pages or the index to 'shine a spotlight' on a particular strategy or Idea.

All of these approaches are perfectly acceptable and readers are actively encouraged to embrace these as part of their active use of the book.

It is recognised that readers may come across strategies or ideas that they already use; this should reassure them that they are currently utilising 'good practice' as part of their story writing provision in the classroom. There may be ideas that readers encounter which they feel will not work with their child authors or will need some adaption or extension to make them suitable for use; this is also considered to be 'good practice' and readers are actively encouraged to not take the ideas presented in this book simply at face value. There are likely to be some ideas that readers will immediately dismiss ('I could do better than that!'). *This is also 'good practice'!* Do use your own creative ideas; after all, this book is not (and could never be) 'the answer' but merely serves as an exciting source of writing stimuli.

It is very much hoped that this book engages not only the children you work with to produce wonderful stories (see Shaw, 2007), but also *you* as a professional in developing and enriching your story writing knowledge and practice. *So go forth... and enjoy stimulating story writing!*

> **Note!**
> At the time of writing all of the *tinyurl.com* links offered in this book were active. As information on the web is regularly changed, updated or removed, it is anticipated that some links may not work for the reader. The author apologises for this, but it is hoped that readers will recognise that this is out of the author's control.
>
> (Brownhill, 2013: 28)

The man sat back in his chair. With all of the cards having been selected there was now nothing left to do but actually write *the book that the* Introduction *had talked about!*

Tap-tap-tap…

Part I

Story elements

Chapter 1

Creating characters!

Being human!

A primary source of 'character' for child authors is human beings. They come in a multitude of sizes and shapes, have different personalities and temperaments, wear various kinds of clothing, and move, talk and behave in exciting and strange ways. Angelou (in Brown Agins, 2006) quite aptly states that this "diversity makes for a rich tapestry". With support from professionals, child authors can easily 'unpick' this tapestry, releasing from it wonderful human characters that can be captured in their own story writing!

Lower Key stage 2

- It is suggested that much of our 'communication' is represented by our body language. Support child authors in exploring the power of non-verbal language by looking at their reflections in mirrors, windows or puddles: *'How can you use facial expressions, gestures and posture to "convey a character"?'* Take digital images of this 'visual language', encouraging child authors to make reference to these when writing about their human character's behaviour as part of their tale of terror e.g. *Kyle threw his arms in the air and shrieked like a moody little girl.* (Toby, 7.7 yrs.)
- Colour is an important consideration when creating human characters – *what colour are their eyes/hair/nails/clothes/skin going to be?* Encourage child authors to create a colour palette for their human characters, selecting colours from magazines, fabrics and painting swabs to represent their personality/mood/temperament: *'Why might they be 'blue'/'black'/'red'/'green'/'white'/'yellow'?'* Use these to enrich character descriptions and their actions as part of a 'colourful chronicle' about wealth, secrets or the ability to read others' minds!

Upper Key stage 2

- Quay (2006: 1) claims that the characters in books she illustrates 'are essentially very human...imperfect, but lovable'. Help child authors to create similar human characters in a 'rooted-in-realism' story by giving them a flaw (be it physical, intellectual or emotional) that makes them of interest to the reader e.g. *they are scared of clowns, they work too hard, they are extremely possessive* or *they have a slight s-s-s-stammer* (think Arkwright from the BBC sit-com *Open All Hours*).

- There is a real danger that human characters can fall into the category of *stockpile* – stereotypical characters such as *Jack-the-Lad* or the *Damsel-in-Distress*. Help child authors to prevent this from happening through careful character planning, creating short 'backstories' or using working-in-role techniques (see http://tinyurl.com/luuqd2s) for professionals and peers to ascertain if characters are a little 'clichéd' for a story involving a modern-day miracle e.g. *a mining rescue* or *the discovery of a cure for all known diseases*.

Gold star!

In order to survive human beings need food and drink. Keeping well fed and hydrated is also of great benefit to their learning, depending, however, on *what* they actually consume (see Ross, 2010)! Make freely available healthy snacks and drinks in the form of fresh fruit, vegetables and water *as* child authors write so that they can '*Drink While They Think*' and '*Nibble While They Scribble*' in an effort to aid the story writing process. Also use food and drink as a stimulus for child authors' story writing – *what happens to human characters when they consume different foods/drinks* (think bananas and Eric Twinge aka *Bananaman*)?!

It's all in the name!

One of the first decisions that child authors need to make is not just *who* is going to be in their story but what *names* they are going to give their characters, especially the lead protagonist (Klems, 2012). Memorable stories contain memorable characters that have memorable names – think of the Artful Dodger (*Oliver Twist*), Tracey Beaker, and Frodo (*The Lord of the Rings*). Professionals can support child authors to select or create names for their story character(s) by using those that are found in baby books, telephone directories, newspapers, holy texts, film credits and street names on maps. Other inspiring suggestions include...

Lower Key stage 2

- Encourage child authors to give their characters either just a first name (*Poppy*), a surname (*Grantham*) or a full name (*Brut Darkvein*). Consider the perceived social status of story characters that have a double-barrelled name e.g. *Emma Hughes-Evans* or a title such as *Dr, Duke, Lady* or *Her Royal Highness*. '*What is the significance of their name at the reading of the Last Will and Testament found in the abandoned cottage?*'
- Suggest that child authors generate nicknames for select story characters e.g. *Soggy, Bubbles, Sparkles, Moonee* or *Mr. Sheen*. Ensure that child authors help readers to understand *how* or *why* characters got these nicknames by writing about the way their characters walk, talk or behave, linking their nicknames to certain characteristics e.g. *they have moist hands (Clammy Chris)* or *they smell of*

damp dogs (Smelly Kelly). 'How do their nicknames change following a fire/dance-off/fight/creative competition?'

Upper Key stage 2

- Talk to child authors about how they can use terms of endearment instead of names when characters refer to close friends and family/those who they love e.g. *Sweetie! Darling! Honeybun! Baby! Poppet!* Consider how these may be used by 'fake' or unpleasant antagonists – think *Cruella De Vil* from *101 Dalmatians* (a great 'play-on-words' name: *cruel* and *devil*) – who try to destroy characters' relationships with others using lies and selfish actions. *'Are their family bonds/love strong enough to keep them together?'*
- Encourage child authors to give 'secretive' characters an alias e.g. *'Mrs. Lacksin'*. Promote the importance of careful story planning to ensure that the real name of the character is not revealed until later on in the story when child authors can reveal *why* they have been given an alias e.g. *they are part of a protection programme* or *they are a spy*. Alternatively, stories that involve fictitious TV/film/pop stars could be given a stage name that aptly describes them e.g. *Diamond*. *'What happens when someone tries to steal their real identity?'* (See Keene, 2009 for inspiration!)

Gold star!

It is not only character names that child authors can have fun selecting or creating; this could also apply to selecting or creating their own! *A Series of Unfortunate Events* by Lemony Snicket is actually the 'pen name', 'nom de plume' or 'literary double' for Daniel Handler. Suggest that child authors might like to write under a pseudonym for stories that are going to be presented on a classroom display (think Parents/Carers Evening) – *can parents/carers/peers work out who actually wrote the story?*

Act your age!

A basic consideration when constructing a character for a story relates to how old the character is. Hardy (2014) suggests that in some cases 'age doesn't matter': is it really necessary to know the age of the *Minions* or *Timmy Failure* (Pastis, 2014)? It obviously helps if readers (and child authors) can relate to story characters in some way; one way of achieving this is by assuming that there is an 'age match'. However, this does not necessarily mean that story characters have to behave in the way their age would suggest – just think of *Gangsta Granny* (Walliams, 2013)!

Lower Key stage 2

- *Grandparent:* Stereotypical descriptions of old people portray them as 'feeble, foolish or inept, passing their time aimlessly in rocking chairs' (Goldman, 1993).

Challenge child authors to write a 'rollercoaster' story (one comprising of lots of 'ups and downs') about a grandparent who defies their age by engaging in extreme sporting activities such as *paragliding*, *snow skating* and *paintballing* – think *Super Gran* (Wilson, 1980)!

- *Adult:* It is generally accepted that when a person becomes an adult they usually start work. Get child authors to identify occupations that they consider to be exciting – think *flying doctor*, *wildlife photographer*, *food critic*, *actor/actress*, *model* or *sportsperson* (Manohar, 2011). Encourage them to write a story in which their story character's job is under threat – think *poor performance*, *cut backs* or *a loss of personal interest* – and the extreme lengths they go to to remain employed e.g. *working 24 hours a day* or *bribing the boss*.

Upper Key stage 2

- *Newborn:* A newborn is defined as an infant who is only hours, days, or up to a few weeks, old. Get child authors to make a collaborative list of things that they can do that newborns cannot: *'Wouldn't it be amazing if a newborn could ride a motorbike, play the flute, build a bivouac or mend a washing machine?!'* Invite child authors to write a mind-blowing story involving an exceptional newborn and their advanced abilities – think *Baby Brains* (James, 2004)!
- *Deceased:* It is said that death comes to all of us. However, rather than story characters embracing their eternal rest, suggest that child authors write a rather unique story that either involves characters living in the afterlife (*Where is the afterlife? What does it look like? What do people do there e.g. sculpt clouds?*) or tells the tale of story characters who come back to life as a different character (think reincarnation – see Tucker, 2013).

Gold star!

Santoso (2009) describes how many great ideas are scribbled on cocktail napkins, toilet paper, and the backs of envelopes, letters and grocery bills due to people 'having no paper to write it down' on. Ensure that child authors are never short of a healthy supply of scrap paper, notebooks, sticky labels, 'shaped sheets', cardboard bookmarks, pads, paper writing cubes, writing sets, journals and 'gem jotters' when writing stimulating stories.

How do I look?

'Writers and readers both agree that, in fiction, one area that is of great importance is good characterisation' (Carter, 2012: 103). One way of achieving this is by making story characters visually distinctive: think *Rapunzel* and her *extremely* long blonde hair; think *Harry Potter* and his thunderbolt scar; think *Quasimodo* and his hunchback. Encourage child authors to give their story characters a distinguishing physical feature that will help to 'lock' them in the minds of the reader (and the child author) long after they have been read (and written)!

Lower Key stage 2

- Get child authors to cut out a pair of large eyes from a self-drawn outline of a character's face (human, animal or fantasy creature); alternatively see http://tinyurl.com/9gyyea2 for a series of eye masks. Invite them to put different coloured pieces of paper / acetate behind the eye holes: *'What effect does this have on your attitude towards the character? For example, are they more attractive? Do you trust them less? Do they come across as warm, cold or mad?'* Encourage them to match characters' eye colour to their personalities, describing why their eyes might squint, dance, sparkle, roll, dart or narrow as part of a vivid story entitled *Those Piercing Eyes!*
- Invite child authors to bring in items of clothing from home that belong to different members of their family. Display these around the classroom, considering what makes them visually distinctive – think *'sharp' (smart)*, retro, *tight, multicoloured, bold print* – or how they could be *made* distinctive e.g. *frayed, stained, with patches, holey / torn, designer logo added, creased* or *dyed another colour*. Get child authors to sketch out a 'visual' of their 'clothed' protagonist for reference, writing an intriguing story which supports or refutes the idea that 'clothes maketh the (wo)man': *'How do your character's clothes reflect / influence their speech / behaviour / actions / moods?'*

Upper Key stage 2

- Offer child authors the PDF from http://tinyurl.com/lsar7vz. On each face outline get them to pencil in different hair styles and types of facial hair e.g. *sideburns, stubble, goatees, moustaches, beards, nose* and *ear* (see http://tinyurl.com/ow2aft8 for inspiration). Encourage child authors to draft rich descriptions of the hair on / around individual faces, commenting on its presentation e.g. colour, amount and neatness. Integrate these descriptions into story passages written to purposefully scare, amuse, surprise or educate readers as part of a story based around a national day e.g. *Sibling, Popcorn* or *Kiss and Make Up* (see http://tinyurl.com/ow2aft8 for further examples).
- Challenge child authors to draw sketches of characters' hands and fingers in response to verbalised descriptions written by professionals or those found in published stories e.g. *The Demon Headmaster* (Cross, 2009). Get child authors to explore how finger nails (*their length and presentation e.g. painted*), size and shape, and jewellery (*type, amount and cost of*) 'accentuate the visual' of characters in their extended story set in a jolly aeroplane or a dreary dairy farm.

Gold star!

Baldwin (2008: 64) recommends that professionals '[e]ncourage students to create unique characters with distinctive features that their readers will be able to visualize'. Broaden child authors' awareness of visually distinctive features by considering one (or more) of the following attributes to make their story characters 'stand out':

Pets (on their shoulder – *parrot* – or under their arm – *dog*)		Glass eye	Posture (do they stand to attention or slouch?)	
Muscles	Eye patch	Broken arm/leg – slings and casts	Big ears (think *Dumbo*)	Chicken legs (thin)
Piercings and tattoos	Hats, scarves and gloves	Beer belly	Yellowing/ white teeth	Enormous bottom (!)
Dreadlocks and bald spots	Disabled – wheelchair	Wearing pyjamas in the day	Masks	Make-up – garish/none
Bags under their eyes	Red rosy cheeks	Glasses/ shades	Jewellery – rings, necklaces	Double/treble chin

Use toys such as *Mr. Potato Head* and board games such as *Guess Who?* to support child authors' understanding and appreciation of visually distinctive character features.

Cultural enrichment!

Ask a child author to talk about/locate one of their written stories that involves characters from different cultures and they might struggle. *Is this because child authors do not see these characters as being 'different'?* Whatever the reason, there remains a limited number of published stories with black and ethnic minority characters, a finding which Laniyan-Amoako (2010) aims to address. With Temean (2010) claiming that 'a writer could add depth to a character if they…include the flavo[u]r of a different culture's background in their writing' it is only right and proper that we encourage child authors to 'bang the drum' for diversity (Blackman, quoted in Ward, 2013) through their story writing.

Lower Key stage 2

- Encourage child authors to promote tolerance and acceptance in their story writing by penning an heart-warming story about a group of culturally diverse children from the local primary school who volunteer to help put together a self-assembly bed for a frail old lady. Promote the use of culturally diverse first names as characters converse with each other (sometimes noisily) when things do not go quite to plan!
- Use the school or local library to research different types of architecture from different cultures e.g. *houses* and *religious buildings*. Invite child authors to set part of their *Indiana Jones*-style 'fast-paced' adventure story in one of these buildings which see characters in a 'race against time' to find and retrieve stolen

treasure/artefacts, returning them to their rightful owner(s) before their mum calls them home for tea!

Upper Key stage 2

- Direct child authors to child-friendly online dialect dictionaries which can be used to convert spoken language between culturally diverse characters in their spy-fiction story, ensuring that their written speech reflects the dialect of the individual speaking. '*What effect does a using different word have in allowing characters to effectively communicate with each other? What happens when the spy turns out to be a parent/guardian?*'
- Suggest that child authors write an informative story which involves them going on holiday (e.g. *skiing, working, safari* or *family*) and making friends with a child who follows a different faith to them. Get child authors to write about interesting situations where they learn from each other about the similarities and differences of their religious thinking and behaviour – think *clothing, customs, beliefs* and *points of view*.

Gold star!

TeachUSWrite (2008) asserts that: '[W]hen it comes to teaching kids writing, one of the most important strategies to teach is how to write a hook. The hook is the very first sentence in the [story], and a good one creates a lasting impression with the reader.' Visit http://tinyurl.com/ndpr8gm to see how the eight identified types of hooks – <u>Question</u>, Quote, <u>Onomatopoeia</u>, Poem, Song, <u>Interjection</u>, <u>Startling Statistic</u> and <u>Dialogue</u> – are combined with pop culture (in the form of *SpongeBob SquarePants*) to really grab the attention of readers! Consider using oral discussion, direct teaching, modelling and focused support to help child authors appreciate the value of appropriate hooks (<u>underlined</u>) in varying the way they 'open' their story.

A little bit 'out of the ordinary'!

It is said that to stand out from the crowd one needs to be a little bit 'out of the ordinary'! If child authors are going to write interesting stories it is important that they think carefully about their lead character, considering ways in which they can make them appealing and intriguing by giving them unusual features and traits. This can be achieved by not only 'observing human nature' (Garber, 2002: 22), be it fictional or real, but also by imitating it!

Lower Key stage 2

- *Speech:* During oracy activities get child authors to experiment with different ways of articulating their ideas with variations to the volume, tone, pace, intonation and expression of their voice. Encourage them think about how characters might talk to others in a written story about a School Bake/Sew/ Dance/Cook/Kick Off, selecting appropriate verbs (see http://tinyurl.com/ kbo7vub) and using visual techniques to represent this on the page e.g. *small text (a quiet voice), ... (a hesitant speaker)* or *$&?! (a character that uses indecent language)*.

- *'Decorations':* An interesting way to create vivid story characters is to 'decorate' them with watches, jewellery, make-up and perfume/aftershave. Work with child authors to consider how cost, quantity, make, colour choice and style help to distinguish their characters from others – think *Hans Moleman's thick glasses (The Simpsons)* or *Captain Jack Sparrow's rings (Pirates of the Caribbean). 'What happens the day after these "decorations" are stolen by the Beautification Burglars? What do characters use as temporary replacements? How are they eventually recovered?'*

Upper Key stage 2

- *Language:* As child authors become more aware of their locality through their Geography studies, encourage them to use the language specific to their region or social group to create a 'home-grown' story character – see *Charlotte's Web* (White, 2003) and *The Railway Children* (Nesbit, 2013). Suggest that they talk to family members to capture written examples of local slang/colloquial speech/idioms/jargon, using these to give their characters' speech an authentic flavour in a mystical story involving gigantic Lego, magic dirt and salty marshmallows!
- *Quirks and mannerisms:* Invite child authors to inflict on a story character a quirk or a mannerism which distinguishes them from others e.g. *saying 'Good!' involuntarily, biting their nails, constantly touching others* or *twitching (eye, head or leg).* Encourage child authors to consider the reasoning behind this quirk or mannerism e.g. *born with it, nervous habit* or *stress-related,* and the effects this has on others around them e.g. *they mimic them, tell them off, sigh* or *are distracted by them.* Use this to energise a VIP story in which characters meet a succession of celebrities, presidents and royalty members by chance.

Gold star!

A team of scientists, mathematicians and creative writing gurus from around the world were asked a question: '"What's the easiest way for a writer to get to know their characters?" Hands down, they all agreed the single best way is to fill out a Character Questionnaire for all your characters' (p. 7). Visit http://tinyurl. com/kfdmkjp, using and adapting the *Character Questionnaire* (pp. 8–10) as a series of prompts (be they oral or written) to help child authors think about their characters before committing them and their adventures to paper. Introduce this idea by getting child authors to collaboratively complete a questionnaire for a well-known character, using hot-seating and interviewing-in-role techniques to stimulate thinking.

Animal-tastic!

There is an abundance of children's stories with animals as central characters; this is clearly evident when one thinks of traditional tales (*The Three Billy Goats Gruff*), Aesop's fables (foxes and tortoises) or beloved children's stories (*Babe*; Joey in *War Horse*). With most children being 'curious about and fond of animals' (Burke and Copenhaver, 2004: 206), professionals are well placed to help child authors to choose interesting animals that serve as lead characters for their own written stories!

Lower Key stage 2

- Suggest that child authors select specific breeds of animal for their stories e.g. *Persian cat* or *a kangaroo mouse*. Provide reference books and age-appropriate websites for child authors to use for research purposes. Get them to think about the country these animals come from. *How do these affect the characters in terms of the language they use, their voice and their mannerisms? How are these evident during a story about a rather stressful week?*
- Challenge child authors to select animal characters that live in particular habitats e.g. *streams, deserts, mountains, ponds, marshlands* and *oceans*. Consider how these habitats serve as a useful story setting for an adventure story involving characters that get lost, caught, fall in and out of love, 'reinvent' themselves as another animal or stumble across eternal wealth, beauty or happiness.

Upper Key stage 2

- Encourage child authors to write stories with animal characters that are now extinct e.g. the *Dodo* or the *Tyrannosaurus Rex*. Consider how 'casting' these animals will influence *when* the story is set. Get child authors to choose two contrasting animals as a 'magical story combination' e.g. *a golden toad* and *a thylacine* [a Tasmanian tiger/wolf] – how do these characters become firm friends despite a clash of personalities during an 'educational epic' or a tale set in two towns?
- Suggest that child authors write a science-based story set in the future about animal characters that have evolved from their present form: *'How have they evolved? What have they evolved into? Why did they have to evolve?'* Encourage them to support their understanding of evolution through web searches for child-friendly information. *'What happens to them the day the Musical Martians land, the sea starts to talk to them or killer rats decide to swamp their home?'*

Gold star!

Consider encouraging child authors in writing interesting stories about animal characters who emulate different characteristics that they are not typically associated with:

(continued)

The 'typically characterised' animal character	The 'newly characterised' animal character	Thoughts and questions
The *proud* lioness	The *shy* lioness	An interesting story title perhaps?
A *shy* koala	A *snappy* koala	Are we talking about a moody marsupial or one who likes taking pictures with a digital camera?
The *snappy* crocodile	The *proud* crocodile	Proud of what? *Her teeth? Her kids? Her tail?*

This can provide child authors with rich opportunities to strengthen and work creatively with adjectives and alliteration in their writing. Extend this by exploring different types of nouns and verbs associated with different animals, considering how inventive variations could create some intriguing new story characters e.g. *a 'bubble of bats'* or *the elephant who 'flounced' all the way to the water hole!*

Fantastical creatures!

Lopez (n.d.) suggests that people in the Middle Ages believed that 'evil spirits, demons and beasts were real and ever present'. Fast-forward some 600+ years and the likes of Rowling (2001), Lopresti (2008) and Allan (2008) continue to delight children and adults with descriptions and images that are the stuff of myths and legends, and even reality (think dinosaurs)! Through the use of appropriate visual stimuli (e.g. *pictures, posters, cartoons* and *film extracts*) professionals can support child authors in developing a desire to write stimulating stories involving invented dragons, fairies, Cyclopes and mermaids!

Lower Key stage 2

* Visit http://tinyurl.com/ne68wrk, encouraging child authors to explore the age-appropriate resources linked to fantasy animals. Suggest that they 'borrow' visual ideas from this website to create a 3D fantastical creature using recycled materials or sculptable art resources (see Sharp, 2000). Use this as a visual prompt to enrich written descriptions of their creature in a 'coming-together' story of two lonely fantastical creatures who become great friends as a result of a journey/discovery/riddle/fire/transformation.
* Download *Fantasy creatures* from http://tinyurl.com/l9f6afm, challenging child authors to name the creatures from the three clues given. Use this as a writing model to help them formulate three key features which distinguish their fantastical creature from others in a fantasy story about a 'Battle of the Brave' competition, a beauty pageant or a foreign language spelling bee.

Upper Key stage 2

- Warber (2014) recommends that child authors should 'think about the[ir] creature's function. Is it a guardian, companion or trickster? ... Does she have special powers? Describe the creature's attitude, emotions, loyalties, interests and dislikes' on a character trait map (see http://tinyurl.com/k5qdobv), weaving these into a harsh story which sees their function challenged or undermined by local villagers, royalty members or the 'vengeful banished' e.g. witches and evil kings.
- Direct child authors to the work of Lange (n.d.) – see http://tinyurl.com/ljn6cef – encouraging them to refer to this to help them create a detailed character profile of a fantastical creature (see *Step 9: Filing*). Share these profiles with peers, challenging them to bring creatures together in a collaboratively written epic story: '*How do their creatures' behaviours* (Step 6) *cause conflict as they embark on a long and difficult journey to defeat the Mirrored Minotaurs or the Slickened Serpents?*'

Gold star!

Think of a die/dice and professionals automatically think of mathematics! *Not so!* Dice can be used as an engaging resource to stimulate child authors' storytelling/story writing. Professionals are encouraged to visit the following websites to aid and assist their storytelling/writing 'dice provision' in their classroom/school:

LKS2	UKS2
• http://tinyurl.com/kypparm • http://tinyurl.com/mv29psp	• http://tinyurl.com/m5dfcrg • http://tinyurl.com/k8bcwc3

The generation-name!

Unfortunately there is no magic formula for helping child authors come up with the perfect story character name, although excessively long character names should be avoided – see *The Boy With The Long Name* (http://tinyurl.com/kkv39mn)! Effective professionals can support child authors by using a range of effective practical strategies such as wordplay, association and rhyme to assist them in generating names for their story characters as the ideas below suggest!

Lower Key stage 2

- Read aloud extracts from myths or stories with a historical setting, changing the names of the characters to popular/'in vogue' ones e.g. *Harry* and *Amelia – does the story still 'work'?* Talk with child authors about the importance of selecting *era appropriate names* to assure story authenticity e.g. *Mabel*, *Fred*, *Ethel* and *Walter* for a story set 'under the stairs' in the Victorian era: '*Why might they want to change their name? To temporarily "escape" the monotony of the extremely hard work they have to do every day?'*

- Encourage child authors to research the *meaning* of character names they have selected, making reference to published books or online sources e.g. *Simon* means 'to hear' or 'to listen'. Get child authors to use this knowledge as the 'fuel' for their character-driven yarn e.g. *why does Simon suddenly stop listening? Is he being deliberately ignorant? Has he 'zoned-out'/'switched-off'? Has he become hard of hearing or temporarily deaf due to an unfortunate happy slapping incident?*

Upper Key stage 2

- Show child authors how to creatively hint at characters' occupations by weaving associated items into their name e.g. Hu**gh Bend**alson (*plumber*), Jenny **Bat**ersby (*professional cricket player*)! Support them in also using these items to create witty (or corny) titles for their stories e.g. *Round the Bend!* or *Blind as a Bat!*
- Talk to child authors about how some surnames have suffixes which offer additional information about the person. Display examples for child authors to use if they wish to write about 'brainy' (academic) characters (*PhD*), lawyers (*Esq.*) or characters who share the same name in a family e.g. Bradley Sanfield *Snr* (father); Bradley Sanfield *Jnr* (son). *'What happens the day these characters suffer a serious injury? How does their life change for the better/worse?'*

Gold star!

If child authors initially 'draw a blank' in naming their character suggest they get on with the actual writing of their story by leaving a gap in the text (if writing by hand) or inserting a line/alphabet letter/series of spaces (if typing using ICT applications) to indicate where the character's name is needed; this can be inserted later on. They may eventually decide to name their character with a *single* letter, particularly when one thinks of the characters Q and M (*James Bond*), Mr. T (*The A Team*) and Malcolm X.

Story writing 'pick and mix' 1

It is personally believed that professionals can *never* have enough learning and teaching strategies and practical ideas for the story writing classroom. To keep story writing fresh and interesting for child authors it is important to engage them with new and exciting ideas to stimulate the writing process and product. This collection of ideas is not attributed to a particular age phase but is offered more as a 'pick and mix' of suggestions for professionals to select from and adapt in response to the writing needs of their learners – *put an 'X' by any that you think you might try out!*

X
↓

Story quotation: A girl was seen in Ipanema wearing a T-shirt on which were printed the words *'Bad decisions make good stories'*. At the plotting stage get child authors to think about the different decisions characters will have to make in their extended story and the subsequent effects of making poor ones.

Story prequels and sequels: We all know what happened to Annabel on *Freaky Friday* (Rodgers, 2003). But what took place on 'Scary Saturday'? What about 'Weird Wednesday'? Encourage child authors to write exciting preludes and follow-ups following a viewing of extracts from the Disney film adaptation.

Story writing races: Engage child authors in individual or paired 'writing races' that encourage them to incorporate new vocabulary (*spelling test words perhaps?*), different types of sentences (*simple, compound, complex*), or use excessive alliteration to make readers giggle e.g. *Peter's plum parrot painted Penny's poppy a peculiar purple!*

Scented stories: Offer child authors to write their stories on scented note paper (purchased or self-made using essential oils, perfume or sprays). Use this to accentuate the focus of the written story being told e.g. *love, gardens, bad smells* or *chocolate!*

Parallel stories: Invite child authors to write two stories, one being a *variation* on the other. Present the stories under each other on the page (as per the illustration), writing one part of the first story and then 'tweaking' it for the second:

| Story 1 |
| Story 2 |

Offer them to peers/parents/carers to determine which story they prefer. 'Tweaked' features could include character names, locations, speech, events and endings.

Story editing: Printed children's stories are always read by different types of editors before they are published. Encourage child authors to take on this role by initially modelling the peer-editing process of their fellow child author's stories – use this as an opportunity to focus their attention on key areas of need (e.g. punctuation or levels of cohesion) or to promote active reading/story sharing!

Chapter 2

Super settings!

Welcome to my home!

The DfES (2001: 5) state that '[b]asing stories in a well-known place is a technique used by many authors'. It is personally believed that there is no story setting more familiar to child authors than 'the home'. The beauty of this as a backdrop for a story means that they do not necessarily have to create the setting seeing as for most of them it already exists! With support from professionals and a little creativity, child authors can use the home as a rich 'base' for some stimulating story writing!

Lower Key stage 2

- Discuss with child authors how the 'safe haven' typically offered by people's homes can be challenged by the weather and the time of day. Write a tense short story in which family members feel unsettled due to noises and occurrences e.g. 'the cold, biting wind which blew deep into the dark, creepy night' (Sammy, 8.4 yrs.) *'What do different family members do in response to these changes – cry? Shake? Hide? Shiver? Hug their teddy/each other? What happens when the weather subsides and the time of day changes?'*
- As a whole group read *Dad's new house* (see pp. 5–6 of http://tinyurl.com/k7snbu5). Encourage child authors to enrich the description of Sacha's new bedroom with sentence strips, using their own or a sibling's bedroom as an internal source of reference. Invite them to 'C&C' the story – *Continue and Complete* it! *'What happens when Sacha is introduced to the new girl? Is Sacha invited into the new girl's house? How does her house compare to Dad's home? What happens next?'*

Upper Key stage 2

- Invite child authors to write a story of misfortunes involving a 'calamitous clear-out' (spring clean) which takes place at their own home. Verbally discuss with others what they would keep, what could be given to charity, and what could be sent to the refuse tip from their bedroom. *'OH NO! What if you accidently put the wrong items in the wrong box? What would you do to try and get back those things that you wanted to keep? Quick – it's a race against time!'*

- At the very end of the 1939 MGM film *The Wizard of Oz* the character Dorothy famously says: 'There's no place like home.' Offer child authors time to think about what makes their home 'like no other place' they know. Consider how they would react if they found that their home had been broken into, caught fire or destroyed in a natural disaster. Write an emotive story about being homeless, living on the streets or in a hostel – think *Street Child* (Doherty, 2009) – or how they, their family and their friends all work together to rebuild their home – see http://tinyurl.com/pwggm2b for examples of powerful emotive language.

Gold star!

With ICT playing an ever important role in our day-to-day lives, it is inevitable that story writing can be supported/enhanced with technological software and resources (see http://tinyurl.com/lfpkgj for adaptable ideas). Provide child authors with access to age-appropriate *story writing apps* (either online- or tablet-based) to aid the story writing process; personal recommendations for professional exploration are offered below, all of which can be found via a *Google* web search:

StoryBook Maker	Story Patch	Toontastic	Story Ideas*	Rory's Story Cubes

* Created by Pie Corbett.

Food venues!

Anderson (2005: 5) succinctly states that 'everyone eats'. With food playing a central role in our lives, child authors should be encouraged to capitalise on this as a 'plentiful plate of possibility' for their story writing. Not only can they set their stories in a variety of food *venues* (the central focus of this Idea) but they can also think about the interesting foods that are *served* there and the *significance* of them to the story, while creating a wealth of story characters with different *attitudes* and *responses* to foods that are consumed e.g. *'Lush!'* or *'Ugh!'*

Lower Key stage 2

- *Coffeehouse:* Initiate a discussion about coffeehouses/shops, emphasising the social interaction where customers might 'congregate, talk, write, read, entertain one another, or pass the time' (see http://tinyurl.com/63qp8s). Make child authors aware of urban storytellers who would be present in Ottoman coffeehouses (see Cizakca, n.d.): *'Imagine you are able to go back in time and visit one of these coffeehouses. Write a recollection story of the tale that you hear being told by the storyteller!'*
- Offer child authors select chapters from *Rude Dude's Book of Food* (Myers, 2014). Invite them to use the knowledge acquired from this as the basis for a stimulating story set in a diner/restaurant/pub/hotel/takeaway venue. For

example, as 'Americans buy one billion dollars' worth of chocolate on Valentine's Day' (p. 11), child authors could write a spirited story about a chocolate-eating competition set in a mall food hall on 14 February. '*What if the winner gets a prize date with the person of their dreams but they turn out to be made of chocolate?!*'

Upper Key stage 2

- *Mobile food trucks:* Show child authors images (web-based) of mobile food trucks. Get them to think about what might be on the menu for a particular type of customer – think *conservative, typical* and *adventurous eaters*. Write a daring story that involves characters being challenged to eat new and exciting foods (think *crocodile, ostrich* and *kangaroo meat*) and the strange effects that they have on their bodies e.g. *they grow fur all over their body, they become as thin as a piece of wire* or *they develop unnatural abilities*.
- *Pop-up restaurants:* Introduce child authors to the concept of the pop-up restaurant – temporary restaurants that are set up in an old factory, warehouse or on a building rooftop. Invite child authors to become a restaurateur for the day – *what would be the style/look/feel/theme/mood/decor of their pop-up restaurant?* Refer to the Internet for ideas. Consider how they would put the above into words, building into their 'day story' events that prove 'challenging' for them e.g. *food poisoning, delayed meals* or *ill chefs!*

Gold star!

There are some wonderful resources available to enrich professional practice when supporting child authors and their story writing. For example, Part 4 of McCarthy's (1998) *Narrative Writing* offers a wealth of fascinating ideas for selection, adaption and application in the classroom. Visit http://tinyurl.com/n5a2xeg, paying particular attention to pp. 41–52: personal favourites include the *story-event map* (p. 45, apt for LKS2) and the *Venn Diagram* (p. 43, apt for UKS2). Alternatively, see pp. 44–50 of the edited work of Rees (1996 – see http://tinyurl.com/lpjynot).

Shops galore!

The Open University (2014) suggests that '[c]reative writing courses and manuals often offer the advice "write what you know"'. A setting that will be known to virtually all child authors is 'the shops'. From frequent visits to the local newsagents to weekly excursions to the supermarket, child authors should be able to tap into a wealth of lived experiences to draw on in their story writing. With so many types of shops offering so many different goods and services, it is surprising that not more shop stories have been written! *Let's get child authors to change that now, shall we?!*

Lower Key stage 2

- Read *Baker Cat* (Simmonds, 2014). Get child authors to rewrite the story set in a *baker's* shop for a more 'mature audience' e.g. their age group, developing aspects of the storyline, building up the characters of the 'mean old baker and his lazy wife' (*why were they like this?*) and enriching some of the dialogue with more naughty expressions! Once complete give the story to a peer to read and pass comment on. *How 'true' is it to the original?*
- Get child authors to imagine that a usual new *bookshop* is to open in their local area – think *on a barge, in a telephone box* or *as part of a barber's*. Unfortunately the shop's stock is delayed in transit and this means that the proprietor is desperate for something to sell on the 'Grand Opening Day'. *Are child authors up for the task of writing a sensational 'Temporary Top Ten' story to line the shelves?* Consider saving this writing activity for *Children's Book Week* or *World Book Day*!

Upper Key stage 2

- Read *A Fly In The Sweetshop* (Dutta, 2003). Get child authors to undertake some web-based research into different types of Indian sweets, writing a culturally based story about a combination of treats that are sold in the *sweet shop* which magically turn the consumer into an actual fly! Encourage child authors to undertake further research into flies so that they can 'inform their fiction' with unusual factual information. *'Don't forget to think about how the consumer turns back into a human being at the end!'*
- Offer child authors a key (real/cardboard cut-out). Tell them it opens the door to a shop that has been left them by an elderly aunt who has passed away – *but what kind of shop is it?* Get child authors to select from a range of shop types – *boutiques, music, butchers, pet, toy, dry cleaners, antique, shoe, sandwich* or *jewellery* – using it as the setting for an extended story of mystery, intrigue and suspense e.g. *what is inside the dusty box that is sat on the counter? Why is the shop 'under threat'? Is there something hidden in the battered safe on the top shelf?*

Gold star!

Grossman (2013) energetically discusses the notion of 'Snapchat Stories' which gives online social media 'users the option to string together pictures and videos taken throughout the day'. As child authors should not register for the likes of *Facebook* and *Twitter* until they are 13 years of age, encourage them to literally 'string together' their efforts using audio recordings (LKS2) and 'face-to-camera' video readings (UKS2) of their written stories. Alternatively, get children to visit and read their stories to younger children in the school (EYFS and KS1); they thus serve as a 'visiting author' to the class!

Sporty locations!

Children are born to move and so sports, or pursuits which involve them being physically active, are important for their development and their health in later life. With many male readers favouring stories that are set within a sporting context – see *Wonder Goal* (Foreman, 2009) – sporty locations offer the perfect backdrop to effectively engage male child authors to *want* to write a stimulating story! This is not to say, however, that it is just boys who like sporty locations – they offer the ideal backdrop to effectively engage both male *and* female child authors – also see *Daisy and the Trouble with Sports Day* (Gray, 2014)!

Lower Key stage 2

• *Leisure centre* – Challenge child authors to set a 'story of peril' in their local leisure centre, using visits or web-based images to consider how the setting presents a danger (potential/actual) to their protagonist's sporting endeavours e.g. *a slippery gym floor to play football on, a tennis ball machine that fires balls at the player too quickly* or *an uneven vaulting horsebox to perform gymnastic movements on*. *'What happens when disaster strikes? How do characters deal with these difficulties?'*

• *Pitches* – Invite child authors to set their story at a particular sporting pitch they know of – think *football, rugby, cricket, hockey* or *boules*. Consider how the pitch and its surroundings help to influence the plot of their sporty story e.g. *poor weather and how this influences the moods/reactions of spectators, tensions between the two teams as there is only one changing room* or *the slowing down of gameplay down due to waterlogged/muddy pitches*. *'How are these tensions overcome/resolved and who are eventually victorious?'*

Upper Key stage 2

• *Outdoor pursuits* – Get child authors to reflect on their experiences while on their residential trip, setting an extended story in or near one of their activity locations e.g. *lake (kayaking), woods (orienteering)* or *archery grounds*. Suggest that child authors consider how stress, nerves and concerns affect their characters (physically, emotionally and/or socially) and their activity performance as part of the 'Ultimate Sportsperson Contest'. *Who manages to ensure these changes do not affect their abilities? How do they achieve this?*

• *Courts* – Invite child authors to locate their 'active story' on a sporting court e.g. *tennis, rounders, basketball* or *netball*. Get them to use rich imagery to enhance descriptions of the location e.g. *the court floor was highly polished, like a pair of new school shoes for the start of term*. Explore what happens when best friends on opposing teams have to compete against each other. *How do they cope with the rivalry that ensues?* *'What happens when unwelcome visitors try to take over the courts?'*

Gold star!

Help child authors by using the Olympics/Paralympics/Commonwealth Games or sporting/activity events that take place at their school as a reference source to 'inform the action' in child authors' sporty story writing – think *sports days, playtime periods, PE lessons, after-school sports clubs, Walk to School weeks* or *Wake and Shake/Activ8*. Encourage child authors to introduce a sporting star (real/cartoon-based) as a character for their energetic story. *'What happens the day David Beckham comes round for a "kick about" or Tom Daly visits for a bit of a splash?'*

Where the 'other half' live!

Altman (2010: 1) asserts that: '[O]n a very basic, biological basis, scientists say we humans are hardwired to be fascinated with celebrity.' Indeed, our love of celebrity magazines, reality TV and celebrity game shows – think *Through the Keyhole* – help to satisfy our desire to see where and how 'the other half' live. The homes of the rich and famous (or well-known) can serve as stimulating settings for child authors' stories as they offer rich possibilities in relation to the *where* (place) element of setting, as highlighted in the suggestions below.

Lower Key stage 2

- Let child authors explore the website found at http://tinyurl.com/7u48clo. Once they have selected a famous person's house, get them to create a collaborative list of 'awesome adjectives' to describe the different rooms they see (see http://tinyurl.com/obe9erb). Challenge child authors to write a fantasy story that involves the famous person in their house, weaving as many of the generated words in vivid depictions of the story setting: *'How does the house change during the earthquake, redecoration undertaken by gnomes or the rising damp fiasco?'*
- Support child authors in creating atmosphere in their 'Day-in-the-Life-of-a-Pop-Star' story by matching character traits to the setting e.g. if a celebrity has a bubbly personality (Alesha Dixon, for example) how is this 'in evidence' in their home? *Lots of fluffy pillows? Warm, bright colours on the wall? 'What happens when their house is surprisingly opened up to the public as a small animal zoo?'*

Upper Key stage 2

- Many American film stars live in areas such as Los Angeles and New York. Get child authors to enhance their description of the condominiums, penthouses, studios and apartments that appear in their extended story about a regrettable wish by considering the weather and temperature. *Is it snowing? Hot? Foggy?* Help child authors to further develop setting depictions by 'including a powerful verb, personification or a simile' (Corbett, 2001: 29) e.g. *The sun beat down…*

The shivering wind sneezed with rain... or *The clouds were as dark as a bruise* as characters deal with the messy outcomes of their regrettable wish.

- If there is an impressive house/building in the locality, take child authors to visit it, engaging their different senses to stimulate 'location writing' (Peat, 2002: 56 – see http://tinyurl.com/mdbnnu8 for more information). *What can they see/smell/ touch/hear?* Encourage child authors to record their ideas by hand on paper or electronically using tablets/digital cameras/dictation machines. Use this information to enrich descriptions of the' story setting in their 'fearsome tale of foe'. *What escapes from the loft? Who terrorises the local primary schools with talking graffiti? Why is there green smoke pouring out of the chimney?*

Gold star!

Efforts to use ICT to support/enhance the learning and teaching experiences of child authors are important to maintain their willing engagement with story writing activity. Visit http://tinyurl.com/kjmr3gn or http://tinyurl.com/4tvzel for a wealth of literacy resources which can be adapted and used by professionals on the IWB or by child authors on individual/shared computers, laptops and tablets – a personal favourite is the *Myths Brainstorming Machine* (http://tinyurl. com/24prev). Consider how these resources can stimulate/support children's storytelling (see Miller and Pennycuff, 2008), which can in turn inform their story writing.

Various vehicles!

Newcombe (2013) claims that that '[v]ehicles and transport are often the centre of great interest from young children'. Indeed, cars, diggers, boats and planes serve as staple toys for children to play with, particularly boys. Support from professionals can help older child authors to locate 'the action' via their stories in a wealth of setting possibilities depending on the vehicle(s) that they choose and where their story characters decide to go in them!

Lower Key stage 2

- Show child authors video footage from the film *Back to the Future* (see http:// tinyurl.com/amql6ug), pausing it to allow them to guess what is inside the truck. Imagine that they win the 'DeLorean-for-a-day' prize at the school raffle. *Where would they go back in history? Why? What do they think they would see/hear/ smell?* Enrich descriptions of these historical settings with explicit reference to 'time' e.g. *morning, afternoon, evening, night, decade, era, century,* BC/AD. *'What happens when the time machine malfunctions?'*
- There are many magical vehicles in fiction that come in various forms e.g. *broomsticks, sleighs, pumpkin coaches* and *ruby slippers*. Get child authors to play the role of a cool inventor who accidentally creates a new magical vehicle – *a Bee Buggie* or a *'Take-to-the-Air' Lampshade* – that whisks them and their friends

to different settings where there are lots of people e.g. *open air festivals, football stadiums* or *concerts*. '*What is it like there? Busy/noisy/hot/smelly/tense/wet?*' Use written descriptions to explain *why* it is like this. '*How do they manage to get back home before the fuel for the magical vehicle runs out?*'

Upper Key stage 2

* Show child authors images of vehicles that can communicate with their owners e.g. *Cars*, Herbie and KITT (*Knight Rider*). Suggest that they write an intriguing story involving a chatty vehicle that serves as an inept travel guide when story characters go on their annual holiday. Stimulate descriptions of the locality with reference to the climate – *tropical/harsh?* – and the geography (physical and man-made) e.g. *mountains, forests, monuments* and *bridges*. '*How are characters rescued from the danger posed by wolves/outlaws/the weather? With the help of flares/helicopters/aliens/floating hearts?*'
* Invite child authors to select plastic letters and numbers from a bag to create the start of the name of a fictional military aircraft (see http://tinyurl.com/3dqy7hs), adding the names of animals to the end to complete it e.g. *JY75 Hawk* or *POH82 Python*. Get child authors to write a powerful warzone story which sees them/their story characters flying into a frantic battlefield to help rescue women/children/animals, presenting their story on long strips of paper which can be spun from the centre on a small electric motor to create the swirling blades of the aircraft.

Gold star!

The National Literacy Trust (n.d.a) describes a *story box* as 'a miniature setting, a shoe box-sized stage with a background and objects within it relating either to a specific book, or to a common story scenario'. Support older child authors in adapting this idea by creating shoebox *dioramas* (see http://tinyurl.com/khlyf9f and http://tinyurl.com/newgwg9 for ideas and guidance) based on the setting of their 'current chronicle', using this to simulate their own and others' story writing. Alternatively, see http://tinyurl.com/ptom9lc for interesting 'ways of interpreting literature with pictures' (p. 1) – personal favourites include *board games, place mats* and *mobiles*.

Places of interest!

Appelcline (n.d.) suggests that: '[I]n previous eras of literature, long descriptions of setting were often admired and respected, but most modern audiences want their stories to get to the action.' While child authors should keep this in mind, it is important that they do not simply ignore their story setting but think carefully about the potential it has to fuel a good story. Story potential can be found in places of interest or tourist attractions, be they local, national or international – if story characters want to visit them it is (almost) certain that *something* will happen to them there!

Lower Key stage 2

- Buildings and structures such as castles, libraries, former prisons, skyscrapers and bridges can offer child authors wonderful locations for their story to take place in and around, especially if they include it in their alliterative title for their tale e.g. *The Clammy Castle, The Loud Library, The Penguin Prison, The Sacred Skyscraper* or *The Butterfly Bridge*. *'What happens the day the contractors come to try and demolish the building/structure? Who/what tries to save it?'*
- A popular place of interest is an art gallery (see Blake, 2015). Invite child authors to imagine they have been personally asked to contribute one of their own pieces of art (2D/3D) by the curator of a gallery. *What would they be willing to have put on show? How do people react to it when they see it? What happens to it during the exhibition?* Write a story about the effect the artwork has on the subsequent life of the artist. *Do they become rich and famous? Do they just experience '15 minutes of fame'?*

Upper Key stage 2

- Signpost child authors to the websites of public aquariums, oceanariums, marine mammal parks and dolphinariums (national/international). Challenge them to write a passionate story in which they and their classmates go on a school trip to one of these places of interest with the secret purpose of setting free the animals that are housed there (think *Free Willy*). *What special things might they have in their rucksacks to help them do this? Do they succeed in releasing the animals or does disaster loom?*
- Petrick (2002) asserts that novelty seeking plays an important role in tourist decision-making. Get child authors to undertake an online search of novelty attractions such as *oxygen bars, the Smallest House in Britain, white-knuckle fairground rides* and *Hamster Land* (purely fictional!). Use one of these as the setting for a particular genre of story e.g. *spy-fiction, romance* or *science fantasy*. *'How does excitement, love or adventure blossom in these environments? Think creatively!'*

Gold star!

It is believed that a popular British playwright kept their manuscripts in the fridge to save them from potential flooding, fire or getting stolen! Invite child authors to find novel places to store their 'work in progress' or 'final drafts' both in the classroom and at home e.g. *in shirt boxes, in between the pages of magazines/programmes, in time capsules, in empty plastic book covers, underneath pillow cases on the bed* or *rolled up inside old shoes!* Alternatively, consider using online storage systems for photographs or digital scans of child authors' stories produced e.g. *Dropbox* and *iCloud*.

International destinations!

Silvey (1995: 449) argues that: '[D]uring the first half of the twentieth century, publishers of children's books made an effort to provide stories about foreign lands.' As such, children now have access to a growing wealth of stories set in countries right across the globe – think *The Firework-Maker's Daughter* (Pullman, 2004). By tapping into, for example, the culture, sights, languages, history, cuisine and music of different countries, child authors can use this to enrich their 'international fiction' (Garrett, 1996) that is set in international destinations.

Lower Key stage 2

- Show child authors select excerpts from Blue Sky's animated film *Rio* (2011), inviting them to work together to verbally generate an array of adjectives to describe the impressive harbour. Use these as part of a magical-mystery story set in the harbour where the Sugarloaf Mountain actually turns into sugar, the Christ the Redeemer statue comes alive and the Carnival takes place with no audible sound. *'How is all this happening? Who is doing this? Why? How are things "put right"?'*
- Play child authors just the soundtrack of footage of the Mumbai flea/street markets in India (visit http://tinyurl.com/lj9pkbt, getting them to close their eyes). Encourage them to capture the hustle and bustle of people selling, bartering and talking as part of a written competitive story about two teams (*what is the gender make-up?*) who are desperate to be the ones to find the 'Crown of Eternal Comfort' as part of a crazy dare!

Upper Key stage 2

- Visit http://tinyurl.com/pcjjfdh, encouraging child authors to select one of the 'Other Culture' videos available on the webpage. Invite them to set their own story in the same location that is visually depicted in the video, writing either a prequel or a sequel to the tale being told. Alternatively, set stories on international shorelines, islands, farms or rural areas that child authors can undertake some online research about. *'How do characters manage to make friends in these quiet locations?'*
- Write the names of different countries on individual tag labels – think of those in *Europe*, *Asia*, *Africa* and *North/South America*. Get child authors to randomly select a label, accessing non-fiction texts to find out some information about their selected country. Challenge them to set a ghost story there, providing enough descriptive passages of the 'locale' so that the reader does not need any illustrations. One suggestion could be to choose a country which 'houses' the modern foreign languages being studied in the school, e.g. France, Germany, Spain and Italy.

Gold star!

Vertsman (2014) offers a wonderful list of children's story books that are set in different countries around the world. Ensure that examples of these are freely made available for child authors, along with non-fiction texts so that they can be used as a constant reference point when trying to capture select elements of the country in their story writing/illustrating e.g. *colours, clothing, smells, dialect, architecture, aspects of faith* and *artefacts*. Alternatively, see http://tinyurl.com/loyn3cq for suggestions on how to develop children's 'writing skills' (p. 15) and creating 'great writers' (p. 16).

The sea and the sky (space)!

Professionals will have little difficulty in being able to name the famous story character who claimed that the sky was falling!* There are many children's stories that have been set in both the sea and the sky (space):

Key stage	Stories set in the sea	Stories set in the sky (space)
LKS2	*The Little Mermaid*	*The Astronaut's Apprentice*
UKS2	*Ottoline at Sea*	Stories from Greek mythology

With the support of professionals child authors can use the vastness that is the body of salt water that *covers* the Earth and the region found *above* the Earth as stimulating backgrounds for their stimulating stories!

Lower Key stage 2

• Share with child authors the story of Atlantis, the legendary city that was supposedly filled with astonishing wealth, knowledge and power that sank beneath the ocean waves. Invite child authors to make believe that they are undersea archaeologists (see Bartram, 2004) who by chance stumble across the city one day. *Where do they find the city? What do they see? Who do they meet there? Are people still 'living' there? What do they find? Is it all a hoax?*

• Get child authors to imagine that they come across a lottery ticket on their way home from school which turns out to be the winning ticket for the £100 million jackpot! With the money they instruct NASA to build them a supersonic space rocket that takes them *up, up, up* into the endless sky… *'What happens when you get up there? Who/what do you meet? Does everything go to plan? How do you overcome any obstacles such as meteor showers, out of control satellites or thick space grime? With the help of Martians/stars/Ground Force Control?'*

* The answer is *Chicken Little*, otherwise known as *Henny Penny* or *Chicken Lickin*.

Upper Key stage 2

- Help child authors to extend their range of locations by suggesting that specific scenes in their tale take place in unusual underwater settings e.g. *sunken ships and submarines, on/in the seabed, lairs, sea plants, inside other animals (think* Pinocchio *and* Jonah and the Whale*), alcoves, deep caves* and *coral*. Encourage child authors to undertake collaborative research into these different locations to bring authentic knowledge into their descriptions/illustrations of characters' surroundings. *'What/who is lurking nearby, ready to pounce?'*
- Lou (2011) claims there are six weird dangers involved in space travel: *space dust, space junk, static electricity, heatstroke, being unable to stop* and...*kidney stones* (yes, really!). Use one or more of these as problems that holidaying space travellers face in an adventure story; these can take place against a vibrant backdrop of asteroid showers, exploding stars, visiting UFOs, black holes and dazzling moons. *'How do these problems affect their holiday?'*

Gold star!

'Enhance the visual' of child authors' stories by providing them with liquid/gel pens and coloured paper (green/blue) to record their stories set in/on/under the sea; for sky (space) stories offer them black paper/card and white chalk/pens. Encourage them to shape their paper with scissors to create wavy, sea-like edges or star/moon/asteroid outlines. Laminate the stories and display them either 'in the sea' (a low, empty/full water tank) or on/from the sky (the ceiling of the classroom). An alternative writing canvas would be on coloured fabric, written using fabric pens. See http://tinyurl.com/q77ddln for some interesting adaptive ideas to display child authors' stories.

Story writing 'pick and mix' 2

Here is a second collection of stimulating story writing ideas to engage child authors and enrich professional practices. As explained in 'Story writing "pick and mix" 1' (see pp. 20–21) this assortment of ideas is not attributed to a particular age phase but is offered more as a selection of suggestions for professionals to choose from and adapt in response to the writing needs of their learners – *put an 'X' by any that you think you might try out!*

X
↓

Story collections: Vary the type of story anthologies that are created in school by classes creating *Story Directories / Calendars / Almanacs / Catalogues / Files*, allowing these to be taken home as part of the school's lending library.
Story entrances and exits: Challenge child authors to devise interesting ways for their story characters to arrive and depart in their narrative (think *Mary Poppins* and Captain Hook from *Peter Pan*) e.g. *through a door made of 'showering' leaves, via an enormous bouncing ball, from the inside of a kangaroo's pouch, into a watch* or *out of a fizzy pop bottle.*
Story mover: Show child authors an iPod / MP3 player or an image of one. Talk to them about this being an 'enchanted portable media player' which speeds up time if the user scrolls forwards / down or slows time down when scrolling backwards / up. Suggest that child authors write a story about the exciting things that they could do if they could accelerate or decelerate the passing of time. *What happens when they press 'Pause'?*
Extreme story writing: 'You've heard of extreme sports, you've probably heard of Extreme Ironing…but what about Extreme Writing?!' Engage child authors in this stimulating activity by varying the locations where child authors write (e.g. *in the toilets* or *on park swings*), the tools they write with (e.g. *charcoal* or *icing*) and what they write about (*stories set on the top of a pyramid* or *stories about people made of cork*). For dazzling extreme writing ideas and prompts see Babbage (2010) and http://tinyurl.com/nr64pwl.
Story colours: Engage child authors by getting them to write their stories using different colours that are associated with the story and its genre e.g. red to represent blood (*horror*), green to represent slime (*science fiction*) or white to represent fairy dust (*fantasy*). 'What happens when the Purple Man / Yellow Lady turn up in the town?'
Story suitcase: Invite child authors to sketch the outline of a suitcase, drawing inside it between five and ten individual random items – think *wooden mouse, bottle top, battery, light bulb, flannel* etc. Challenge them to write a captivating story in which each of the items is needed / used by a new arrival at Hogwarts, by Second World War refugees or by Blyton's *The Famous Five.*

Chapter 3

The plot thickens!

What have you lost?

A universal experience which we can all relate to is losing something or someone: *'Do you know where Sally's reading book is?'*; *'I've misplaced my keys!'*; *'Roger Rabbit is not in his hutch, Mum!'* The inability to find something or someone typically serves as the trigger for a story in which characters go in search for 'the lost'. Work with child authors to consider what could be missing in their 'lost and found' story – *Shoes? Artwork? Treasure? A diary? A tooth?* – and when/where/if/how story characters eventually find it!

Lower Key stage 2

* Technology plays an ever important role in our lives. Suggest that child authors write a 'techie' story about a character that loses their smartphone/tablet/laptop/ MP3 player/handheld games console. Consider ways in which this item becomes lost – *it is misplaced, stolen, hidden, moved, thrown away* or *dropped* – and how the character's life is temporarily affected by its loss – *positive/negative? 'How does the story end? Do they find the lost item or not? Why/not? What do they learn as a result of this?'*
* Invite child authors to thought shower different occasions when people use money e.g. *paying for a meal in a fast-food restaurant, purchasing a comic, splashing out on a new football/gymnastics kit.* But what happens when a character reaches for their wallet/purse and their cash/cards are not there? *How do they react? What do they do?* Get child authors to write a 'story of panic' that explores the different emotions their characters go through as they strive to retrieve their 'lost dough'. *'Where has their money gone?'*

Upper Key stage 2

* Show child authors a blank *Lost Pet* sign (see http://tinyurl.com/okunp5f; p. 2) as an example). Get child authors to work in pairs with one child author writing an emotive story about how an *owner* tries to find his/her lost pet, and the other child author writing an emotive story about how the *pet* tries to find his/her lost owner. Support them in bringing the two stories together at the end via a poignant finale. *Are the owner and pet finally reunited?*

- The loss of a friend can be painful; this could the result of falling out with one another, growing/drifting apart, or death – see *Michael Rosen's Sad Book* (Rosen, 2011). Encourage child authors to write a sad story which details not only the events that lead up to the loss of a friend, but also the events that occur after this e.g. *characters having a period of mourning, characters making new friends, characters moving on/away. 'Is it true that time is a healer?'*

Gold star!

Vandergrift (1997) asserts that it is worth remembering that: '[Y]oung people are creators as well as consumers of literary works.' Help child authors to *feel* like *real* authors by publishing (displaying) their story writing on writing walls (LKS2) and on school websites (UKS2). For further ideas see http://tinyurl.com/kddkp43 and http://tinyurl.com/ye7wf9e. For practical suggestions as to how to use displays to support story writing in the classroom see http://tinyurl.com/qdzo88d (pp. 2–10).

Family (mis)fortunes!

Many child authors will have heard of, watched and even played the game *Family Fortunes*. Add the prefix 'mis-' and they are likely to generate rich stimuli for their stories; indeed, Despeaux (2012) argues that misfortune can 'make your writing stronger'. The first *Golden Rule of Story Writing* (see http://tinyurl.com/p9a23xl) states: *Don't Bore Your Reader!* With this in mind, challenge child authors to spice up their stories with interesting struggles, encounters, disputes, fights, quarrels and clashes for their families (real/imagined) to endure!

Lower Key stage 2

- Get child authors to write a list of all of the different activities they have engaged with at home and at school from the moment they woke up to the point where they are writing the list e.g. *brushing teeth, eating breakfast, walking to school, reading*. Get child authors to write a story about the day their fictional family open a Chinese *mis*fortune cookie resulting in them all being tremendously accident prone all day – *how might lived experiences* (such as those detailed on the list) *support the story plot e.g. do they get a nasty paper cut while reading?*
- Suggest that child authors write a story in which different family members all 'come down' with different illnesses at the same time e.g. *colds, the flu, measles* and *whooping cough*. Encourage child authors to research the ailments and treatments of each illness in an effort to develop their subject knowledge and understanding in terms of how story characters try to care for one another, presenting this learning through the vehicle of 'a sensitive story'.

Upper Key stage 2

- Offer each child author a folded raffle ticket, reading out each number so that every child author in the class 'wins'(!). *But what do they win?* A chance to write a creative story about a family who win a 'gigantic prize' at the school tombola, that's what! *But what do the family actually win? 'That is up to you!' Does the family want the prize when they see it? Why/not? What happens when they take it home? Do the family's feelings towards it change over time? Why/not?*
- Boyce (2012) highlights a number of different types of misfortune e.g. *housing problems, noise, family turmoil* and *violence*. Encourage child authors to select one of these 'difficulties', considering the physical/emotional/spiritual/mental effects that this has on different family members. Explore how wider family members help those in difficulty as part of their exploratory story – think *giving hugs, talking, making plans* and *confronting the situation 'head on'*. *'What are the effects of these different actions?'*

Gold star!

The Golden Rules of Story Writing (see http://tinyurl.com/p9a23xl) offer child authors and professionals a number of relevant and valuable rules to 'keep in mind' when writing stories:

1. *Don't Bore Your Reader!*	2. *Be Clear*	3. *Show, Don't Tell*	4. *Be Original*
5. *Get Inside Your Characters' Heads*	6. *Structure Your Story*	7. *Rewrite, Rewrite, Rewrite!*	8. *There Are No Golden Rules*

Use the guidance offered on the website to actively support child authors' story writing, encouraging them to create their *own* rules for story writing (with support where necessary) in light of Rule 8 above!

The quest!

Quests are a wonderful plot device for children's stories – they serve as a journey that protagonists go on in search of someone or something, be it tangible e.g. *hidden treasure, money* or *'powerful' jewellery* or intangible e.g. *fame, advice* and *love*. Quests typically engage the reader because they involve story characters encountering 'a maze of awe, disappointment, dangers, delays, and experiences' (Durand, 2007) which helps to sustain their interest; this also applies to the child author who decides to write a story that is driven by a stimulating quest!

Lower Key stage 2

- In real life we do not always win; talk to child authors about Captain Scott's ill-fated expedition to the Antarctic in 1912 or about the original ending of the film

DodgeBall (2004) which shows the protagonist's team failing to win the final of the tournament. Suggest that they write *two* different endings to a pirate quest story, one where the pirates *succeed* and one where they *fail* in claiming 'their' treasure. Invite peers and parents/carers to read both endings and choose which one they prefer with oral reasoning. See Montgomery (2006) for inspiration.

- Those on a quest rarely do it on their own: they usually have a faithful companion(s) by their side – think Frodo's Sam (*The Lord of the Rings*) and Dorothy's Tin Man *et al.* (*The Wizard of Oz*). Encourage child authors to create a faithful companion for their 'quester': *'Is the relationship between the 'quester' and companion(s) always supportive and harmonious? When/how/why is it put to the test?'* Help child authors to discuss how companions are introduced by writers in published quest stories so that they can structure their own writing accordingly – see http://tinyurl.com/psrrx9q for useful background information.

Upper Key stage 2

- It is important that near the end of a quest lead characters have some kind of epiphany (*self-truth*) e.g. they realise something about their life, their culture, their way of thinking or behaving, an example of which might be that they love each other (think *Shrek* and *Princess Fiona*). Help child authors to give their writing a key purpose – to educate others through some 'lessons learned' – by ensuring their story characters 'come out the other end' of their quest a stronger/wiser/kinder/changed person. Make reference to http://tinyurl.com/ovgtya9 for support.
- Encourage child authors to sustain reader interest in their quest by introducing small sub-plots e.g. *characters are kidnapped/rescued/die/fall in love/make a dreadful mistake/give up/lie about something/reveal their 'true colours'.* With reference to the current class story book, visually show child authors how sub-plots 'work' by drawing a tree trunk outline to represent the main storyline and 'branches' of other stories (sub-plots) that connect to the main storyline. Encourage child authors to weave at least one sub-plot into their own quest – *can peers 'spot it'?!*

Gold star!

Professionals are encouraged to take a look at the following websites, videos and e-book samples about story quests, selecting academic information and ideas which can be adapted for use in their story writing classrooms:

Quests (website): http://tinyurl.com/qyrqo3d	*A Step by Step Guide to Writing Stories with E.R. Reilly!* (video): http://tinyurl.com/qgq64wa
Writing the Hero Quest (website): http://tinyurl.com/63wa93a	*Story Quest: Creative Writing Guide for Story-Writing Workshops* (e-book sample): http://tinyurl.com/qj5rh3d

What's that you've found?

An interesting way that child authors can develop the plot of a story is by having their lead character find something, be it an inanimate object e.g. *a message in a bottle* or *a sign*, or something living e.g. *a person*, *a creature* or *an animal*. Their character's 'finding' could be deliberate or it could be by accident, stumbling across it purely by chance. Stimulate child authors' story writing by getting them to be explorers in the classroom, actively rummaging or foraging about for hidden/surprise items. Alternatively, get them to *imagine* things that they/their story characters could find, not only in the classroom but in locations outside their place of learning. *What if they found the following:*

Lower Key stage 2

- *Magic powers?* What 'houses' the magic powers? A shell? A cushion? A glue stick? What can the magic powers do? Are the powers used for good – why/not?
- *A purse/wallet?* What is inside it? Who does the purse/wallet belong to? How do you know? How/is it returned to its owner? What is special about the purse/wallet?
- *Food?* What sort of food is found? Is it expensive or cheap food? Is there enough for everyone to try some? What happens when people eat the food?
- *The head teacher?* Where are they hiding? What/who are they trying to hide from? How are they found? Do they hide often? Why?
- *A mobile phone?* What sort of phone is it? Who does it belong to? Who could be on the other end of the line when it rings? How does 'the receiver' react to the call? Is the news good or bad?

Upper Key stage 2

- *A key?* What is the size and shape of the key? Is it heavy or light – what is the key made out of? What does the key open/unlock? *A door? A box? An old chest?* What is special about the key? Who does it belong to?
- *A handwritten note?* What does the note say? Who has written it? When was it written and why? What happens when the note is read? Where is the note found?
- *A mouse?* Where has the mouse come from? Is the mouse lost or is the mouse part of an infestation? What/how does the mouse try and communicate with the 'finder'?
- *A shoe?* Who does the shoe belong to? Where is the other shoe? When were the shoes worn last? What is special about the shoe?
- *A gold coin?* Where was it found? Where did it come from? *Italy? India?* How much is it worth? What could it be used to buy? Are there any special markings on the coin – what do they mean?

When writing their story, encourage child authors to think about how their story character reacts when they find something: *are they surprised? Elated? Scared? Astounded? Glad? Shocked? Intrigued? Joyous? Horrified? Relieved? Thrilled? Puzzled? Excited?* Support child authors in developing the 'emotional range' of their characters' reactions by making reference to visual emotion charts (facial expressions), online word lists or using 'emotions' dice, spinners, photographs and puppets (see Fox and Lentini, 2006). *'What do characters do with "the found" once they have found it?'*

Gold star!

In *Lost and Found* (Jeffers, 2005) the penguin finds friendship in the boy. Help older child authors to appreciate things that their characters could find that are not tangible e.g. *companionship, the truth, one's voice, happiness, inner courage, love, strength of character, peace* and *faith*. With support, encourage child authors to consider how their lead character(s) could 'find' these non-tangible entities through their experiences and encounters with other individuals, be they both positive and not so positive.

Open sesame!

There are many stories which involve characters opening something – think *a chamber (Harry Potter and the Chamber of Secrets)*, *a box (Pandora's Box)* and *a cave (Ali Baba and the Forty Thieves)*. The repercussions of doing this help to 'fuel the plot' (Hadley-Garcia, 2013) and satisfy the reader's curiosity with regard to finding out what is inside! Encourage child authors to weave into their story an object or item which is opened (see examples below), reminding them to think about what happens as a result of these objects/items being opened!

Lower Key stage 2

- *Window.* Who opens it? *A witch? An alien?* How is it opened? *Flung? Slowly? Hesitantly?* What flies out of it? *Birds? Clothes? Paper planes?*
- *Car.* What kind of car it is? Where does it stop? Who steps out of the car? *A film/pop star? A VIP? Your teachers?* Where do they go/does the car go?
- *Washing machine.* What comes out of it once the washing cycle has finished? *Music? Balloons? Crockery? Flowers?* What is hidden in the bottom of the drum?
- *Magician's cabinet.* What appears when the smoke clears and the cabinet is unbolted? *A tiger? The thief? A talking kettle?* What/who is hiding in the secret compartment?
- *Drawer.* What is inside the drawer? *Gold? A smartphone? Keys? Mum's handbag?* Is the drawer stuck/locked/broken? Why?
- *Food packaging.* Does the food inside match the label? Is there something living inside the packaging e.g. *mice?* What is special about the packaging? Who tries to steal the discarded packaging? What do they use it for?

Upper Key stage 2

- *Email.* Who is it from? When was it sent? What does it say? What does it contain? *A document? Pictures? A video?* What is the reaction of the receiver?

- *Coffin.* What size/shape is it? What is it made out of? How is it decorated? Who/what is inside it? *A skeleton? Lost treasure? Eternal light?* Is it buried or 'above ground'?
- *Text message.* Who has sent it? When was it sent? What does it say? How does the recipient react to it? Are there any emoticons/photos attached?
- *Toilet.* What leaps out when the lid is lifted? *A bunny rabbit? A serpent? A panda?* What is hiding/being hidden in the cistern?
- *Loft hatch.* What falls out of the loft as the hatch is opened? *A bike? A time machine? A dangerous book?* Who/what has eaten through one of the cardboard boxes stored up there?
- *Voice message.* Who is the message from? When was it left? What does the message say? Is it good or bad? What if only half of the message has been recorded? What did the other half say?
- *Suitcase.* What is inside? *Someone else's clothes? Stolen money? A will? A ration book?* What has happened to the lock/handle/combination/clasps/straps?

Support child authors in making their story a surprising experience by adding pop-up paper features to their illustrations, thus enhancing the 'reveal' aspect of their object/item. See Irvine (2005) for practical ideas on how to increase the complexity of the paper engineering, depending on the abilities of the child authors and the confidence of professionals!; alternatively, see http://tinyurl.com/qzll2r3 for book presentation ideas.

Gold star!

Visit http://tinyurl.com/now2shc for a wonderful PDF full of Foldables by Zike (2008). Consider the potential of using these with child authors to stimulate their story writing e.g. encouraging child authors to write their stories on differently designed Foldables (pp. 8–9). Alternatively, visit http://tinyurl.com/6e9podx or http://tinyurl.com/ps7qjzj for further ideas and suggestions in relation to story writing which can be adapted for the child authors you work with.

The fear factor!

Roddy (2003: 3) advocates the three-step method of 'a tangible Objective, some Obstacles and the Outcome' to help child authors 'shape a story idea into a finished narrative'. An obstacle that almost everyone can relate to is that of fears (*feeling afraid*) and phobias (*intense levels of fear*). There are many things that can frighten us and these offer child authors a real 'wealth of possibility' when thinking about what their story character's fear or phobia is (*the obstacle*), what their *objective* is (to face or overcome their fear or phobia perhaps?) and how they try to overcome it, the *outcome* being whether they succeed or not.

Lower Key stage 2

- Children's fears become more realistic as they get older, examples of which include *injury, illness, school performance, death* and *natural disasters* (Smith *et al.*, 2014). Challenge child authors to write a story about a character's fear of *public speaking* in the context of 'giving a report in class, speaking at an assembly, or reciting lines in the school play' (Lyness, 2013). Support them in carefully story planning several story attempts that fail before their character eventually succeeds in overcoming their common fear.
- Situational phobias (those that are triggered by a specific situation) include a fear of *enclosed spaces (claustrophobia)*, *flying, driving, tunnels* and *bridges*. Build child authors' appreciation of backstory by thinking about the *cause* of their story character's phobia (most likely from an adverse childhood experience). Model how child authors can present this to their readers in their story by writing a dream, a flashback or a memory recall episode.

Upper Key stage 2

- Through their reading experiences encourage child authors to make a note of the fears that different story characters have and how these relate to the theme of the story e.g. *a fear of failure/change/being unloved/hurting others/looking stupid/ rejection/the unknown* or *conflict*. Encourage child authors to consider how these fears mirror their own, using this to inform a 'partially-based-on-a-lived-experience' story in which child authors can supplement their 'fact' with embellished and entertaining fiction.
- Smith *et al.* (2014) suggest that one phobia type relates to Blood-Injection-Injury: '[T]he fear of blood…injury…needles or other medical procedures.' Encourage child authors to create reader empathy by offering rich descriptions of their character's 'overwhelming anxiety or panic…intense need to escape', loss of 'control', feeling like they are 'going to die or pass out', or knowledge that they are 'overreacting, but feeling powerless to control [their] fear' when faced with an operation. *'How can you get readers to really "feel" your characters' pain? Think sweating, heart palpitations, feeling clammy, light-headed and being sick!'*

Gold star!

Soar Higher (2006: 1) proposes a technique called SOAR to help people develop accomplishment stories that can be told to showcase their skills in interview situations. This can easily be adapted to offer 'structural support' for child authors when verbalising/writing their own stories:

SOAR stories	Story writing using SOAR
Situation: Describe the situation.	**Situation:** Talk/write about the 'story situation' e.g. who is in your story and where it takes place.
Obstacles: Describe the obstacles you faced.	**Obstacles:** Talk/write about the obstacle(s) your character faces.

SOAR stories	Story writing using SOAR
Actions: List the actions you took.	**Actions:** Talk/write about the actions of your character in response to the obstacle(s) they face.
Results: Describe the results you helped obtain and the benefits to your organisation.	**Results:** Talk/write about the results of your character's actions and the benefits of these to themselves and others.

Model the use of this to help child authors see the value of using SOAR to help them structure their written stories.

Rescue me!

Dictionary definitions of the verb 'to rescue' emphasise the idea of setting free or saving someone or something from danger, attack, imprisonment or death. 'The rescue' is a common plotline in stories and films and is typically characterised by 'the hero' rescuing the damsel in distress – think *Superman* saving Lois Lane or Prince Phillip rescuing *Sleeping Beauty* with a kiss. Child authors can use 'the rescue' as a stimulating driving force for their own story, particularly as they can be creative with regard to *who* or *what* is going to be rescued and *how* and *why* the rescue takes place.

Lower Key stage 2

* Share with child authors short written descriptions from non-fiction books about hazardous locations e.g. *the sea, mines, caves* and *mountains. 'What rescue services are available to help those who get into difficulty in these different settings?'* Encourage child authors to set their rescue story in one of these locations, undertaking web research to develop their knowledge of the rescue service, the location and possible accidents that can happen there. *'What if it is the rescue service that has to be rescued?!'*
* Williams (2011) talks about the rescue plot as being a three act story: 'Separation, pursuit, confrontation and reunion.' Use this as a simple aide memoire to ensure that child authors plan and structure their rescue story appropriately. Encourage them to work on each 'act' separately to help focus their attention over the writing week: *'How could you use a "reunion" to start the story? Think family, class, military, club, neighbourhood or business!'*

Upper Key stage 2

* Encourage child authors to embrace a 'role reversal' in their story writing by putting a female character in the role of the rescuer – see the end of the film *Enchanted* (2007). Make reference to http://tinyurl.com/olvs3mn to see how Lansky is keen on children writing a rescue story that 'showcases a main character [female] that is clever and courageous (rather than witless and helpless)'.

'How will you get your female protagonist to demonstrate qualities such as bravery, determination, ingenuity and strength (personality/physical)?'

- Get child authors to imagine that it is *they* who have to be rescued in their rescue story. Encourage them to write their story from their personal perspective, imagining what they think their rescuer might be having to do to help rescue them. When they (the child author) are finally saved – *how/when/by whom?* – how does the 'imagined' rescue compare to the story eventually told by the rescuer (the second part of the story)?

Gold star!

Create a series of rescue prompts (words or images presented on individual cards) to help those child authors who require some inspiration to 'kick-start' their thinking with regard to writing their rescue story. Examples might include:

Lost	*Flood*	*Chains*	*Shark*	*Trapped*
Fire	*Illness*	*Storm*	*Pit*	*Dungeon*
Ghost	*Kidnap*	*Spaceship*	*Plane*	*Prison*
Tree	*Lock*	*Train*	*Magic spell*	*Kiss*
Criminal	*Evil Doctor*	*Tied up*	*Fall*	*Broken*
Gagged	*Fight*	*Pipe*	*Dragon*	*Hostage*
Alien	*Car*	*Cave*	*Bully*	*Cage*
Witch	*Explosion*	*Bus*	*Blindfolded*	*Cliff edge*
Hole	*Battle*	*Well*	*Cell*	*Wizard*
Boredom	*Dinosaur*	*Sinking Ship*	*Volcano*	*River*

Other rescue prompt cards can be created by child authors themselves in response to their talk about/reading of rescue stories (those in fiction books or reported in the news).

Didn't I warn you?

The 'warning story', as Corbett (2008b) explains, follows a simple pattern: 'the tale hinges on a warning being ignored'. This clearly guides the plot of the film *Gremlins* where the strict instructions of the Chinese shop owner – *do not expose Gizmo, the lovable Mogwai, to bright light, get him wet or feed him after midnight* – are overlooked with disastrous results! Encourage child authors to use their own experiences to fuel their warning stories, particularly as 'Didn't I warn you?' is likely to be something they have heard many a time from parents/carers and professionals 'after the event'!

Lower Key stage 2

- Get child authors to imagine they hear on the radio one morning the DJ warning of a mysterious 'enchanted storm' that is about to hit the area where they live.

Ignoring this results in everybody...*well, that's for child authors to decide!* Spend time as a group focusing on unusual ways in which individuals try to help others underdo the effects of the storm e.g. *saying 'Pimply bottoms!' backwards five times, biting one's toenail with their eyes closed* or *pouring honey into their belly button!*

- Read *Do Not Open This Book* (Muntean, 2006). Invite child authors to write their own adaptation of the book as an anniversary special, using their 'creative writing licence' to present a new lead character, new events and some invented language that is used to write it – see http://tinyurl.com/mnndboq for information.

Upper Key stage 2

- Suggest that child authors choose one of the warnings which frequent the mass media e.g. *the concerning amount of 'screen time' children spend in front of TVs/laptops/tablets, rising obesity levels in children, stranger danger* or *global warming.* Use this as the basis for a 'side-by-side' story in which *two* stories are written *alongside each other* on the page: Story A tells a tale where the warning is ignored, with Story B telling the same story but details what happens when the warning is noted and acted on. *'How could the stories come together at the end?'*
- Get child authors to test their knowledge of warning signs through a simple game of recognition (see http://tinyurl.com/nxtm8ks). Invite them to select one of these signs and use a description of it to 'open' an extended story. Carefully consider the reasons why story characters dismiss the sign – *arrogance, illiteracy, bravado* or *a dare* – and whether one of the lead characters actually survives the traumatic ordeal that ensues.

Gold star!

The 'warning tales' of the Brothers Grimm – think *Little Red Riding Hood* and *Hansel and Gretel* – have both delighted (and frightened) children for over 200 years (see http://tinyurl.com/og2mof7 for other story examples). Using NBC's police drama series *Grimm* as the inspiration for this idea, work with child authors to modernise select fairy tales for the twenty-first-century reader with reference to up-to-date fashions (*hoodies*), music (*R&B*), popular culture (*taking a selfie*) and technology (*Wi-Fi and iPads*). Alternatively, see Robinson (2005) for some 'mixed up' inspiration!

Making mistakes!

Cleaver (2006: 22) claims that a useful 'plot trigger' for a story involves a character making a mistake. Published children's story titles such as *Snake's Mistake* and *The Fairy's Mistake* highlight how errors serve as an effective catalyst for an interesting written story. Encourage child authors to initially talk about mistakes that *they* have made, either at home or at school. Create a verbal/written list of these so they can be used to stimulate their own and others' stories. Over are some possible examples.

Lower Key stage 2 – 'Slip-ups'

- Saying the wrong thing at the wrong time in a School Council meeting.
- Not shutting the animal cage door properly.
- Pressing the wrong button on the smart phone/TV remote/kitchen appliance.
- Crossing the road without looking both ways.
- Passing the wrong message on from a received telephone call.
- Putting items of clothes on the wrong way.
- Singing the wrong words to the song in assembly/the choir.

Upper Key stage 2 – 'Blunders'

- Falsely accusing someone of doing/saying something they did not do/say.
- Forgetting to click 'Save' when typing up their homework.
- Performing the wrong musical scale during a music lesson.
- Writing down instructions in the wrong order.
- Mishearing a comment made by a friend/peer.
- Putting the wrong amount of ingredients into the cake bowl.
- Miscalculating a percentage in a maths exam paper.

Berkun (2005) suggests there are four *types* of mistakes people make, many of which are relevant to child authors in KS2:

- *stupid* [silly] e.g. stubbing a toe;
- *simple* e.g. having the electricity go out in the middle of a house party because Dad forgot to pay the bill;
- *involved* (mistakes that are understood but require effort to prevent) e.g. regularly arriving late to school every day; and
- *complex* (mistakes that have complicated causes and no obvious way to avoid next time) e.g. relationships with others (friends, family members, girl/boyfriends) that fail.

Use the above to help child authors to categorise the different mistakes they write about. Through focused taught input ensure that child authors appreciate that *everyone makes mistakes* – it is part of being a human being! This also applies to the characters in their stories; readers will find protagonists who never make any mistakes 'too perfect' and rather boring. It is therefore important for characters to not only *make* a mistake(s) but also try to *rectify* their wrong doing(s). This might involve them:

Sincerely apologising for what they did/said	Offering some penitence e.g. being upset, writing letters of apology
Taking responsibility for their actions and admitting they made a mistake	Putting in place practical strategies to ensure that mistakes do not happen again

Adapted from Cottringer (2005)

Talk with child authors during PHSCE opportunities about practical ways that they can rectify mistakes they make in their work and their relationships with others to support their story writing e.g. *be honest, listen to what others have to say, try harder next time, act on your errors, double check things, avoid situations where easy mistakes are made, concentrate and do not rush* and *think before you act*. Bring these strategies alive through the use of drama – see http://tinyurl.com/mchm4r6 and http://tinyurl.com/kqmpcjz.

Gold star!

In *The Girl Who Never Made Mistakes* (Pett and Rubinstein, 2012), Beatrice Bottomwell learns that it is not possible to be perfect all the time. Help child authors to develop their story endings by encouraging them to write about the 'lessons learned' by their characters from the mistakes they make e.g. *not to do 'X' again, always put a coat on when it is raining, think before you speak, take your time* or *never laugh at others' misfortune!* Relate this to other well-known story characters e.g. Naughty Amelia Jane and Perfect Peter (from the *Horrid Henry* series), considering if/how they change as a result of their mistakes.

Story writing 'pick and mix' 3

Here is a third collection of stimulating story writing ideas to engage child authors and enrich professional practices. As explained in 'Story writing "pick and mix" 1' (see pp. 20–21) this assortment of ideas is not attributed to a particular age phase but is offered more as a selection of suggestions for professionals to choose from and adapt in response to the writing needs of their learners – *put an 'X' by any that you think you might try out!*

X
↓

	Story Post-its®: Invite child authors to write a story about a story book full of Post-it® notes. These are secretly inserted into the book on which are written different challenges devised by a vengeful story character that dislikes the reader. *What are the challenges? Does the reader take up the challenges? Do/how do they succeed?*
	Self-standing stories: Offer child authors two pieces of card to create a criss-cross stand by cutting a slit in both pieces and slotting them together: Use the eight faces to either present eight short stories, four longer stories (one story across two faces) or one extended story across the eight faces.
	Designer stories: Research reported by Unicef (n.d.: 4) highlights how children are increasingly aware of the designer labels worn by 'the rich'. Satisfy the potential materialistic streak of child authors by writing a story which *weaves* designer label names into the very 'fabric' of the story e.g. *Ralph [Lauren] lived with his friends Tom [Ford], Paul [Smith], Hugo [Boss] and Louis [Vuitton] in a big mansion high up in the Hollywood hills.*
	Letter change stories: Suggest that child authors write a wacky story about talking cereal, petulant pillows or holidaying suitcases and then change individual letters in the names of characters and settings. *How does this change the story?* For example, Dawn could become **Y**awn which is her nickname because she is always sleepy; her house could become a **M**ouse, a large plastic model in which Yawn lives at the local fairground!
	Story errors: Recommend that child authors write a farcical story about a 'jelly nightmare' with deliberate errors in it, be they spellings, character 'switches' or continuity issues e.g. the shades worn by Ben suddenly become green even though they were described in the previous sentence as being black. Invite fellow child authors to 'de-error' the story – *how many 'story slip-ups' can they find?*
	Story about a story: Challenge child authors to write a story about a child author who decides one day to write an extended story. *What happens to them during the writing of the story?!*

Chapter 4

Colourful conflict!

It's all in my mind!

One of the two main types of conflict in story is *internal conflict*. Sometimes referred to as *self-* or *intrapersonal conflict*, it describes the struggle that takes place in a character's head. This is evident in the verbalised thoughts of Charlie Brown in the comic strip *Peanuts*: 'I feel terrible! I hate myself!!' (see Rubin, 2012). Support child authors in developing their use of internal conflict in their story writing, revealing this through their use of 'dialogue, narration and a character's actions' (Hickman, 2014) when making difficult choices or decisions.

Lower Key stage 2

- Internal conflict is evident when a character is *indecisive* e.g. *which route should we take to get to the Cottage of Chaos? Shall I have vanilla or chocolate-flavoured ice cream for breakfast?* Encourage child authors to write an exploratory story about 'Indecisive Isaac/Isabella', exploring ways that they practically learn to overcome their indecisiveness by making decisions in their everyday life e.g. *picking out their own clothes, choosing food for tea* or *packing their own rucksack for school.* Use conscience alley (see http://tinyurl.com/p9zs6t3) as an engaging drama tool to verbally generate the indecisive thoughts which go through the character's head which can be used to inform the written tale.
- Read extracts from *The Suitcase Kid* (Wilson, 2006). Talk to child authors about a character's *divided loyalties* as a result of a divorce. *Which parent should they spend their birthday/Christmas with? How do they tell their dad that their mum has a new boyfriend and that they* [the character] *like him?* Get child authors to explore how their story character wrestles with these divided loyalties in their story about 'living two lives' (one with mum and one with dad), emphasising the emotional difficulties they experience to elicit sympathy from the reader. **Note:** Do remember to be sympathetic to child authors' own personal backgrounds when engaging with this writing activity.

Upper Key stage 2

- *The Adventures of Huckleberry Finn* (Twain, 2009) offers many examples of a character *struggling with his conscience* e.g. *when he wants to learn to smoke* and *when he helps Jim to seek his freedom.* Challenge child authors to write a love story in which their lead character struggles with their conscience but ultimately recognises 'the difference between right and wrong… [is] able to empathize with others, feel…remorse when causing an other's pain, and ha[s] the capacity to inhibit behavio[u]r that is unlawful or unethical' (Frazier, 2001) as part of their efforts to win their love's affection.

- Research by NICE suggests that 'in the last decade there has been a steep increase in the number of primary school children suffering signs of depression' (cited in Donnelly, 2013). Invite child authors to write a sensitive story based around a character who shows symptoms of depression, exploring some of the possible influences for this – think *pressures from social media and cyber-bullying*, *school testing* or *being perceived as overweight* – and how family and friends rally round and help them to cope with the troubled voice they have in their head.

Gold star!

Gold star! suggestions usually offer professionals a single, quality idea; this one offers 30! Visit http://tinyurl.com/nbyeh9 for 'a variety of eclectic, classroom-tested techniques' related to the teaching of writing taken from full-length articles published by the *National Writing Project* in America. Personal favourites include Ideas 8, 10 and 20. Consider ways of adapting these techniques to suit the age group/needs of those that you work with.

Intense illnesses and injuries!

Baudet (2013) asserts that a '[c]haracter against illness, [be it a] parent, friend or self' serves as an interesting *external* form of conflict. All child authors will experience some form of real-life illness (a cough or a cold) or injury (a bruised elbow or a 'bumped' head). With support they can draw on this to help them write a stimulating story which *could* (hint hint!) explore the challenges that characters must confront, manage and (hopefully) overcome when they or others are poorly/injured.

Lower Key stage 2

- The DC Comic book character *Peter Parker* was famously bitten by a radioactive spider, resulting in him turning into *Spiderman*. Get child authors to consider other 'biting' animals that could turn characters into a different superhero e.g. a dog (*Dog Boy*), a lion (*Lion Lady*) or a chinchilla (*Chinchilla Chap*). Support child authors in developing detailed descriptions of how characters fall ill once they have been 'nipped' prior to their transformation e.g. *they might sweat, shake, shiver, collapse* or *vomit* (ugh!). *'What happens to them as a superhero?'*
- 'Spotty' characters can be used by child authors to elicit powerful moods and emotions from both readers and other characters in a story. The spots could indicate *chicken pox, measles, rubella, a rash, blisters* or simply *acne*. Consider how other characters react to those with spots (*disgust, sympathy, surprise* or *fear*

– see http://tinyurl.com/q8kvmsl for further examples) and how 'spotty' characters strive to recover from them e.g. *positive thinking, bed rest, taking prescribed medication* and *prayer*. '*Do they become a "beautiful swan" at the end of the story (think* The Ugly Duckling*)?*'

Upper Key stage 2

- Unfortunately in some stories characters die as a result of their illness – think of *Tiny Tim* when *Scrooge* is visited by *The Ghost of Christmas Yet to Come* (Dickens, 2008). Encourage child authors to write a *commemorative story* which looks back at heart-warming/heart-breaking events in the life of their character who passed away as a result of a chronic illness (see http://tinyurl.com/qyc29zo for inspiration).

- Challenge child authors to rewrite Dahl's (2007) *George's Marvellous Medicine* in an effort to address the underdeveloped plot and somewhat abrupt ending which were some of the criticisms of the book when it was first published. Get them to rethink the role of Grandma's original medicine in helping her recover from a 'fake' injury she claims she sustained from a fall, a fire or a driving accident. Help child authors to experiment with *multiple* endings to their redraft to actively engage the reader (see R.L. Stine's *Give Yourself Goosebumps* series).

Gold star!

Morris (2013) claims music to be 'an odd facilitator for writing'. Offer child authors access to a range of different genres of *sound stimuli* (see http://tinyurl. com/najmfqy) in the classroom, either *before* they write (e.g. listening to 'The Aquarium' from *The Carnival of the Animals* by Saint-Saëns prior to writing an story set under the sea), *during* their writing (e.g. new-age music – think Robert Haig Coxon – to inspire and relax child authors), or *after* they have written (as part of the discussing/rereading/redrafting process).

Competitive streak!

Cantador and Conde (n.d.: 1) suggest that: '[I]t is controversial whether competition in education is positive or not.' While there are fors and againsts for its use, competitions serve as a rich source of conflict to stimulate story writing – just think of the mileage J.K. Rowling got out of the Triwizard Tournament in *Harry Potter and the Goblet of Fire* (2004)! With trials suggesting that introducing a competitive edge to school mealtimes could increase the number of children eating fruit and vegetables by a third (Belot *et al.*, 2014), it may be possible to raise engagement and quality levels of story writing in the classroom by a third by weaving a competitive streak into the 'story mix'!

Lower Key stage 2

- Get child authors to create a list of as many different races as they can that take place during a school sports day e.g. *sack*, *egg and spoon*, *skipping*, *three-legged*, *wheelbarrow* and *relay*. Get child authors to write a spirited story in which different 'houses' compete against each other to try and win the prestigious Silver Shield: *'What devious tactics do different characters deploy to disadvantage the opposition e.g. using itching powder, putting butter on batons or mildly electrifying ropes with batteries?'*
- Show child authors a picture of your imaginary/real best friend. Talk about them being the most popular person you know and how *everyone* wants to be their friend. Get child authors to think of different ways story characters could compete to be best friends with popular people using *money, flattery, invitations, gifts, laughter, support* and *conversation*. *'Whose genuineness shines through though in the end?'*

Upper Key stage 2

- Tell child authors about a new TV show which is in development called 'The Fame Game'. The premise of the show measures the lengths that contestants will go to to achieve fame and fortune in a short time period. Invite child authors to write a lively story in which two rival contestants try to outdo each other by doing extreme things to attract mass media attention: *'What ridiculous things do they do to try and increase their popularity? Swim naked with sharks perhaps? Is this popularity long lived? Is fame everything?'*
- There are many online story writing competitions child authors can enter (visit http://tinyurl.com/om3jzvt for suggestions). Encourage child authors to enter one of these with a story *about* a competition between story characters. Get them to reflect on how their obsessive competitive streak affects their lives (positively/not so positively) in terms of their friendships and relationships with others e.g. peers and family members.

Gold star!

Dough Disco is described by Bennett (2014: 4) as:

> a daily activity which combines the use of pieces of dough with a series of hand and finger exercises. These strengthen and develop children's fine and gross motor dexterity, hand-eye co-ordination, proprioception [the body's ability to sense movement within joints and joint position], balance, low load control, grip and most importantly, their self-esteem!

Visit http://tinyurl.com/q63r4yj to see Shonette Bason energetically demonstrating her Dough Disco concept! Ideal for the EYFS, consider ways to adapt this for child authors, particularly for boys who are physically 'pained' by writing in KS1 and KS2 (Wilson, 2013), in terms of the movements made, the music selected and the material to manipulate!

Antagonistic animals!

It is well argued that conflict is essential to plot as without it there would *be* no plot (Brownhill, 2013)! A common form of external conflict present in children's stories is that of 'man versus man' e.g. *two rival female football teams battling it out for the Golden Cup.* 'Man versus man' does not just mean human beings; animals can serve as a living form of conflict – think *Rikki-Tikki-Tavi* (Kipling and Davis, 1992). With this in mind, invite child authors to thought shower all of the animals they know with drawn sketches and/or words, select one and 'consider the conflict' that they could present to fuel a super story!

Lower Key stage 2

- Show child authors short extracts of the Pixar film *Finding Nemo* where Marlin and Dory 'come into conflict' with dangerous animals of the deep blue sea e.g. *barracudas, sharks, sea devil fish* and *jellyfish.* Support them in writing a story where they replace these lead characters with their own protagonists – *'Who are they and what are they doing in the sea?'* – considering how they creatively overcome the conflict presented by these different antagonists.
- Consider purchasing the wonderful *Conflict Animals Deluxe Set* (see http://tinyurl.com/nfzxegx), exploring with child authors the different conflict styles described/exhibited by the different animals. Use one of these as the basis for a 'struggle story' between two animal groups, detailing how they creatively overcome their natural conflict style to eventually 'win' using ingenuity, thought, bravery, magic, team work and/or persistence.

Upper Key stage 2

- Introduce child authors to the literary technique of *foreshadowing* which is described as hinting at things to come. *'Think of it as a kind of a warning or a tease for the reader!'* Exemplify this through the retelling of *Cinderella* (see p. 1 of http://tinyurl.com/kcsxvml), supporting child authors in developing foreshadowing conflict between humans and animals in their contemporary fairy stories e.g. *rumbling tummies* (hunger), *angry verbal 'vents'* (revenge), *brewing storms in the sky* (imminent attack) or *silent birds* ('the calm before the storm'). See http://tinyurl.com/pljwdj5 for useful background information about foreshadowing.
- Get child authors to think about an inappropriate animal for a pet. 'Set the story scene' by describing how their evil Uncle Snarl deliberately buys an untamed animal for their family as an early Christmas gift. Generate as a group humorous or frightening 'goings-on' which cause much angst for different family members in response to the animal's antagonistic behaviour – *think whether it is really their fault that they behave in this way!* *'How do the family tame or eventually get rid of the animal?'*

Gold star!

Download the PDF at http://tinyurl.com/o63uscv which offers a series of conflict bookmarks that can be used by professionals to help child authors build up their understanding of different types of conflict when reading published stories and the written work of their peers. Consider adapting these for different ages and abilities of child authors through the use of pictures and images, space for drawings, tick lists, questions, prompts and visual reminders. Alternatively, get child authors to create their own conflict bookmarks!

Technological turbulence!

It is argued that conflict 'must exist for the story to exist' (see http://tinyurl.com/pvrqca3, p. 1). This 'makes the story move' (p. 1) and one source of conflict to assure this movement comes in the form of technology. This appears in a lot of science fiction stories and cartoons – think *The Iron Man* (Hughes, 2005) and *Transformers* (cartoons and films). When child authors 'place...a character against man-made entities which may possess "artificial intelligence"' (p. 2) – think *machines*, *robots*, *gadgets* and *computers* – rich story potential then exists (see Beaty, 2013; Gall, 2013).

Lower Key stage 2

- Get child authors to imagine that (Step)Mum/Dad has decided to 'Rent-a-Robot' for the day. *What does it look like? What size is it? What is it called? How does it communicate?* Invite them to create a large sketch of the robot, plotting their story *inside* the drawing. *'What is the problem with this robot? Is it a killer robot? Does it steal things or lie? Is it defiant or clumsy?'* Suggest that child authors present their story using ICT applications for a display using an appropriate 'technology' font e.g. Lucida Console or OCR A Extended.
- Place an iPad (real/image) on a large sheet of floor paper and invite child authors to think about all of the things that they use this piece of equipment for, offering these thoughts on the paper. Get them to then 'animalise' the item (a bit like 'personify'), considering different ways it might try to defend itself from being actively used – see http://tinyurl.com/pnyzzof for ideas. Weave these ideas into an imaginative 'defensive story' called *The Indignant iPad!*

Upper Key stage 2

- Create a mobile made of old CDs/DVDs, inviting child authors to sit and gaze at it in a darkened classroom with torches directed at it. Verbally offer them the opening of a story which sees them receiving a CD or a DVD through the postal mail. *Who sent it? What does the disc contain?* Get them to continue the story in written form, building story tension by considering the adverse effects caused by playing the disc/surveying its content or being pursued by dangerous hi-tech androids who seek the CD/DVD which they constantly refer to as 'The Her-heart'.

- Get child authors to imagine that the IWB in the classroom serves as a gateway to new and exciting yet hazardous worlds inhabited by antagonists in the form of *Yakkers* (mobile phones that talk you to death), *Teblets* (tempestuous tablets) and *Zippers* (cars that travel at breakneck speed). Invite child authors to write a thrilling story about entry to one of these worlds using one of Tobias' (2012) *20 Master Plots* to give reasoning to the entry (also see http://tinyurl.com/q5qzutw for some really excellent checklists linked to these).

Gold star!

Horn (n.d.: 1) argues that: '[L]earning the role of view point and understanding that each person has a unique point of view (POV) is one of the most important thinking skills that a child can acquire.' Read Horn's interesting article on POV and the PDF that is available at http://tinyurl.com/l8o7quz, using role play and questions (apt for LKS2), and POV stories and video clips (apt for UKS2) to help child authors learn how to link the events in a story causally (Emery, 1996).

Wild weather!

Jones (2014) claims that the '[w]eather has played an important role in many military operations throughout history. The timing of the D-Day invasion [for example] was heavily influenced by weather forecasts and conditions.' This 'important role' is also evident in many well-known stories – think *Noah and the Ark* (rain) or *The Wizard of Oz* (tornado). With a wealth of weathers available to choose from, child authors should be encouraged to use the weather to stimulate their written stories.

Lower Key stage 2

- It is suggested that 'describing the weather' helps to make a good ghost story (see http://tinyurl.com/pc74mt7). Encourage child authors to use a range of interesting adjectives – *the menacing dense fog; the whipped whistling wind; the smudgy grey rain* – to help enrich the dark atmosphere and add to the tension that is needed before the ghost *('What does it look like?')* makes its first terrifying appearance.
- Believe it or not, red, yellow, black and green rain has actually fallen from the sky (see O'Sullivan, 2012: 10–13)! Invite child authors to write a special story that involves coloured weather e.g. *purple clouds, orange blizzards* and *pink dust storms*, exploring how these are created. *'What effect do they have on the lives of the characters who encounter them? How long do the effects last for?'*

Upper Key stage 2

- Lee and Fraser (2001) describe rainbows as a natural phenomenon, noted for their beauty and presence in mythology. For creative child authors suggest that they turn this enthralling multicoloured arc into a vicious sky serpent which 'slinkies' its way across the land, causing mayhem wherever its lands. *'What is it looking for? What happens if/when it finds it? What happens to it after that? How do story characters try to "do battle" with it?'*

- Invite child authors to combine types of weather to create a 'weather-blend' e.g. *sun, hailstones* and *thunder; sleet, ice* and *tornadoes.* Challenge child authors to write a story in which this 'blend' serves either as a form of transportation for escapees, a villain's weapon, the result of a piece of amateur magic at a school fair, or an unusual backdrop which the story action plays out against.

Gold star!

Help child authors to quickly recognise increasingly difficult high frequency words and build their levels of accuracy when learning spellings by presenting words with the initial and final letters written in a different colour e.g. readiness; dreadful. Alternatively, present the letters that child authors miss out/get mixed up with *within* words to help focus their attention e.g. receive, February. For less able child authors, visit http://tinyurl.com/pufrg9g for information, resources and links to 'a fun system' called *Rainbow Words* to support the learning of letters/sounds, sight word recognition and spellings.

Challenging environments!

A key source of external conflict in stories comes in the form of the physical environment. This is supported by the Balance Publishing Company (1989: 1) who define 'Man against Nature' as 'a character [who] struggles with the elements'. Exemplification of this can be found in the work of London (2013: 1) where the protagonist 'wants to live, but Nature, in the form of the barren arctic tundra, stands in his way. To survive, he must overcome all that Nature puts in his way: an injured ankle, hunger, cold, distance, wolves, etc.' *What interesting challenges can the environment throw at story characters in the hands of your child authors, I wonder?*

Lower Key stage 2

- Offer child authors a small, sealed, bottle of water. Let them experiment with making the water move in different ways, promoting appropriate vocabulary to describe this e.g. *undulating, vortex, crashing, spraying, wavy* and *pulsating.* Encourage child authors to integrate these words into a story of survival set in the ocean (*which one?*), considering the challenges the sea and creatures of the deep present for shipwrecked passengers, pesky pirates or sea-sick sailors.
- Read select poems from *Space Poems* (Morgan, 2006). Get child authors to think about the challenges of living up in space as an astronaut for a year – think *loneliness, meteors, space pirates* and *solar flares* (see http://tinyurl.com/n626b2s for inspiration). Offer child authors black paper on which they can write in white chalk/crayon a story of how Annie/Andy the Astronaut deals with these difficulties. *Do they become friends with the space pirates? Do they learn to 'ride' meteors? Do they ever get home?*

Upper Key stage 2

- Offer child authors the following rich story starter: *As I walked into the cave...* Get them to thought shower the difficulties characters would face if they chose to stay in the cave for a period of time in an effort to raise money for charity – think *toileting, heating/cooling, food and cooking,* and *humidity control.* Visit http://tinyurl.com/pxpd6ej, reading and adapting ideas from other authors to add further conflict into the 'story mix' e.g. *supernatural goings-on, technological failures* or *internal struggles with perseverance.*

- Give child authors select extracts from *Jungle Tangle* (Thomas, 2013). Challenge child authors to continue the story, introducing problems that threaten the health and safety of the protagonists – think *mosquitoes* (malaria and yellow fever), *contaminated food and water* (fever, diarrhoea and dehydration), *leeches* and *small, venomous creatures* (snakes and frogs). *'How/do they survive their different ordeals? What happens when the tigers plan a co-ordinated attack?'*

Gold star!

Maynes and Julien-Schultz (2011: 194) argue that graphic '[o]rganizers provide cognitive structures that support learners' ability to relate ideas and support critical thinking and higher levels of cognition'. Visit http://tinyurl.com/nej548t, considering how the graphic organisers presented on pp. 4–8 could be used to make 'abstract concepts more concrete' for child authors to think/write about in their stories e.g. *time, being free, good and evil, love, success* and *morality.* Alternatively, use these to help child authors develop an understanding of story structure – think the *Story Mountain*!

Forces of nature!

Man versus nature is considered to be one of the most basic forms of conflict in a story. This 'nature' can be on a small scale – Rosen's (1997) *swirling-whirling snowstorm* – or a large one – think of the flood in the biblical story of *Noah and the Ark*. The challenge for child authors is to purposefully put their story characters in a situation where they come face to face with a natural disaster influenced by Mother Nature! *But which disaster to choose from* (see http://tinyurl.com/l5lbhk) *and what happens next?*

Lower Key stage 2

- Invite child authors to make a large origami boat (see http://tinyurl.com/d9nlxmv). Use this as a piece of 'plotting paper' for a story involving characters who inadvertently sail headfirst into a blizzard. Ensure that they give rich descriptions of the strong winds, heavy snowfall and low temperatures which characterise a blizzard. *'How do the characters manage to keep warm on the boat? Do they survive/does the blizzard subside?'*

- Provide child authors with a range of musical instruments, encouraging them to make the sounds that they think they would hear during an earthquake. Suggest they integrate these sounds in written form into their 'disaster' story in which their characters' escape route from the hotel / compound / stadium / forest is continuously fraught with shaking and ground ruptures causing road / bridge damage and the collapse of buildings: *'Do they manage to escape with their lives?'*

Upper Key stage 2

- Challenge child authors to write a 'race-against-time' story involving characters who get caught up in an avalanche. Get them to consider what these characters were doing before the avalanche hit – *are they snowboarders / skiers / snowmobilers?* – and how their actions (possibly) contributed to the onset of the avalanche. Spend time thinking about atypical rescue teams – think *aliens*, *animals* and *ghostly spirits* – and how they rescue the characters in the nick of time.
- Suggest that child authors use their story writing skills to 'warn' (educate) others. Ask them to write a 'who-dun-it' story in which a forest / wild / bush fire occurs and the threat that this poses to wildlife and human inhabitants. Work with child authors in offering subtle hints about what caused the fire. *Was it as a result of a volcanic eruption, arson or human carelessness?* 'Are readers at the end of the story able to clearly say why children should never play with matches?'

Gold star!

The use of varied writing paper, in terms of its colour and shape, can be stimulating and performance improving for child authors (see Winter and Winter, 2009: 3). Continually offer them paper of different hues, tints, shades and tones (see http://tinyurl.com/3mmvqj2 for information) which can be shaped by child authors in response to key aspects of their story e.g. objects (*paper shaped into a chocolate box*), settings (*a dome to represent a character who lives in the* Eden Project) or characters (*paper shaped like a pair of outrageous sunglasses*) to engage them with their story writing.

The menacing supernatural!

Think 'the supernatural' and many immediately think 'scary'. Indeed, while there are educators, parents [/carers], and political and religious institutions who consider supernatural stories 'disturbing or harmful to children' (see Dawkins in Knapton, 2014), Taylor (2010: iii) asserts that '[c]hildren's fascination with monsters is a normal part of childhood development'. Support child authors in considering the conflict that 'mysterious force[s] or being[s], representing things beyond rational scientific explanation' (Misra and R, 2012) can provide for their written 'fearful stories'!

Lower Key stage 2

- It is widely assumed that all angels are good. *Not necessarily so, especially when in the writing hands of child authors!* Support them in developing a 'fallen angel', one who causes conflict for the story character who discovers it hiding in a box of old Christmas decorations. *'How does it prevent them from working/enjoying a holiday/sleeping at night/exercising? How does the story character manage to overcome the influence/power of the angel?'*

- Talk to child authors about *The Birds* (du Maurier, 2004) which Alfred Hitchcock made into a famous horror film. Get child authors to consider an alternative animal(s) which suddenly and without warning starts attacking people and buildings with their claws/eggs/food/waste. Get them to consider why the animals are doing this, how this affects the day-to-day lives of people, and how the animals are eventually eradicated. *Poison? A bomb? A bolt of lightning? A flood?*

Upper Key stage 2

- A classic supernatural antagonist comes in the form of Bram Stoker's (1993) *Dracula*. Support child authors in adapting the tale, considering alternatives to the blood that he so desires at night e.g. *sweat, tears, mucus* or *saliva. 'If the story was set in your home town what problems would this vampire cause for different inhabitants that you know? How do inhabitants manage to find out the vampire's "alternative" weakness e.g. he hates hearing Taylor Swift's music or cannot stand being near cottage cheese?'* Waa-ha-ha!

- The life of a superhero is fraught with conflict with supernatural villains. Encourage child authors to undertake some research into antagonists (male/female) created by *Marvel* and *DC Comics*, adapting action verbs to create their own superhero e.g. *Target, The Gobbler, Execute. 'What is their problem with* Plastic Man/Silk, *for example? How do they attack them and how does the good guy/girl manage to eventually defeat them?'*

Gold star!

Noodlehead tales are described as 'light-hearted tales about silly people doing silly things' (Chen, 2014). Visit http://tinyurl.com/ckbfmvf, encouraging child authors to write stories about crazy characters drinking tar, trying to walk on the ceiling or licking doors and humming! Add to the purposeful silliness by deliberately 'relaxing' spelling, grammar and punctuation conventions as the story is written. *Perhaps child authors could try and write their story using their non-dominant hand?!*

Story writing 'pick and mix' 4

Here is a fourth collection of stimulating story writing ideas to engage child authors and enrich professional practices. As explained in 'Story writing "pick and mix" 1' (see pp. 20–21) this assortment of ideas is not attributed to a particular age phase but is offered more as a selection of suggestions for professionals to choose from and adapt in response to the writing needs of their learners – *put an 'X' by any that you think you might try out!*

X
↓

Story maze: Get child authors to draw a series of individual images on a piece of paper e.g. *a ring / shoe / pen / cup of tea / car / postcard* or images taken from magazines / junk mail. Connect these together with circles and lines to create a visual maze. Invite child authors to 'write their way' out the maze by producing a story which links all of the items together (see Wright, 1997: 106–108 for more details).
Self-writing story: Invite child authors to write a story about a tablet, laptop or PC which becomes a best-selling author by writing stories all by itself! *'What happens when the true identity of the author* (Dell Latitude 6430u) *is eventually disclosed to the publishing world?'*
Story watching: As part of a school trip / visit build time into the day for child authors to quietly sit and 'soak in' all that is around them. *What can they see / hear / touch / taste / smell* (within reason!)? Get them to create a visual 'cue' of items of interest (drawings / digital images) which can be used to stimulate stories they write when they get back to the classroom.
'Special' stories: Suggest that child authors write stories for a unique audience who have *never* had a story written for them before e.g. *a tap, a bottle of water, a handbag* or *a shoe!* Get them to think about what would potentially engage these 'listeners' / 'readers', integrating this into the written tale e.g. *money, dodgy clasps, dog paws, messy make-up* or *vibrating mobile phones (handbag).*
'Fine' stories: Just like fine food and fine wine (i.e. fine dining) introduce child authors to the notion of 'fine' stories – stories which are written with the finest (*well thought through*) ingredients (*elements*), constructed with the greatest of care (*plot*) and physically written (*handwriting*) with love, thought and pride. Present completed 'fine' stories on a specially reserved display board in the classroom for others to aspire to.
Story jumpers: What if story characters could 'jump' from storybook to storybook when lined up next to one another on the library shelf. *What wonderful tales could be created if story characters 'mixed'?!* Let's write and see!

Chapter 5

Resolving the problem/s!

Forgive and forget!

Research by Jose and Brewer (1983: 20) found that the 'liking of [a] story's outcome was determined by resolution of...a positive ending for young children and by the just world ending for older children'. One ending that can resolve the conflict in some stories is to 'forgive and forget'. There are many stories found in the Bible associated with the theme of forgiveness (see http://tinyurl.com/pjunfd9) – consider using these as a starting point to help child authors understand forgiveness as a decision/ process/response for use in their stimulating story writing.

Lower Key stage 2

- Get child authors to thought shower examples of sibling rivalry, disobedience or difficult friendships (either lived experiences or from fiction they have read). Select one of the ideas generated, writing a reflective story which carefully plots a combination of different situations that result in characters 'distancing' themselves from each other. Explore why one character decides to 'close the gap' that has formed between them by forgiving and forgetting what has happened for the sake of their friendship/relationship/others.
- Signpost child authors to http://tinyurl.com/pu4xlnv, encouraging them to select and read one of the many stories available on the website about forgiveness. Help child authors to download the PDF available at http://tinyurl.com/nmdkglj, adapting the activity described so that an embellished retelling of their chosen forgiveness story from the 'Stories of Forgiveness' collection is presented on the heart instead.

Upper Key stage 2

- Visit http://tinyurl.com/ms7y39w, giving child authors the opportunity to familiarise themselves with the story of *The Golden Deer*. Challenge them to write a detailed contemporary version of the tale, using colloquial phrases, references to pop culture and a looser version of the plot to entertain and educate a modern-day audience about forgiveness. Alternatively, rewrite the story within the context of a different faith.
- Introduce child authors to the 'Five steps for granting the gift of forgiveness' as set out by Klimes (see http://tinyurl.com/nwfwp52). Encourage child authors to write

a supportive story which contextualises these five steps for the reader, integrating story flashbacks to describe different situations which resulted in the protagonist unfortunately feeling betrayed – think *broken promises*, *addictions and obsessions*, *avoidance*, *revenge* and *anger*. Exploring unfamiliar Aesop's fables and Anansi stories may offer child authors some useful ideas.

Gold star!

The Narrative Activity Pack (Calderdale & Huddersfield NHS Trust, 2012: 3) 'provide[s] practical ideas and resources for use at home and at school' in developing the narrative abilities of children. Download the pack from http://tinyurl.com/loq4rt3, considering the value of using activities advocated by the Trust to teach lower ability child authors about *question words*, *sequencing* and *time*. Encourage them to apply this knowledge when they are writing their own stories. Alternatively, see http://tinyurl.com/q9glp47 for some useful *Talk4Writing* resources for use across the full Key stage.

Seek help!

LifeCare (2011: 4) suggests that: '[T]here may be times when, despite your best efforts, you may not be able to resolve a conflict on your own. If so, get help.' While professionals should actively encourage children to 'sort it out themselves' in an effort to build skills of independence, there will be occasions when they will need to request the assistance of peers, siblings and adults to constructively deal with situations that they cannot resolve themselves. This can be positively modelled through their story writing!

Lower Key stage 2

- Encourage child authors to play select *Travel Games* (Kemp and Walters, 2003). Invite them to write a story about a holiday journey (by car, coach, plane or train) in which these games are played yet there is conflict between individuals due to them being overly competitive. Consider who is playing and who they seek help from to resolve the tension which is built from this game play e.g. *parents/carers*, *siblings*, *friend*, *driver*, *pilot* or *steward/stewardess*. '*How is the conflict eventually resolved?*'
- Write the first names of boys and girls from different cultures separately on pieces of paper, inviting child authors to select two (a boy and a girl). Get them to write a cultural-based story in which the extended families of these two story characters get together for a celebratory meal (*Birthday? Festival? Special holiday?*) and the two main story characters are told to 'go and play together': '*What conflict is generated from this forced pairing? Why does it occur? Who do they seek to resolve the conflict? Siblings? Aunties/uncles? Step-cousins? Godparents? How is the conflict eventually settled?*'

Upper Key stage 2

- Show child authors a world map and get them to select a country. Invite them to create an imaginary penfriend from the chosen country whom they regularly email (a type-friend). However, get child authors to imagine that the penfriend has recently started sending unpleasant emails – *'What are they about? What makes them "unpleasant"?'* – and the child author does not know what to do about it. *Whom do they seek the support of to address this problem?* Discuss with peers practical ways that this conflict could be resolved, selecting the best/most appropriate idea for their international story.
- Get child authors to think of as many themes for a birthday party as possible in two minutes – *GO!* (see http://tinyurl.com/cl5f76 for suggestions). Suggest that they create a small 'story cast' that attend the party but who dislike the theme/are bored by it/hate having to get dressed up. *'How do they express this through their body language/actions/speech and how does this make the birthday boy/girl feel?'* (consider using role play where appropriate). Explore who is called upon to address this conflict to ensure that the party is an eventual success e.g. *the party planner, parents/carers, siblings, family members* or *the 'entertainment' e.g. clowns, magicians* or *DJs*.

Gold star!

Professionals can never have enough stories to tell and child authors can never read/be told enough stories! Fire their writing imaginations with a wide range of stories (Hopwood-Stephens, 2013). Super online sources to extend professionals'/child authors' known bank of morally-based stories include:

• *100 Moral Stories* – see http://tinyurl.com/n62mjs2 (apt for LKS2)	• *Short Stories for Children for Spoken English Program* – see http://tinyurl.com/nd9or6w (apt for UKS2)

Using physical force!

One way to manage conflict is through physical force. This approach is understandably discouraged by schools who actively promote the development of children's verbal conflict resolution skills (Coleman *et al.*, 2014), and this Idea does not *in any way* attempt to challenge this quality practice. Within a 'safe' story writing context, however, professionals might suggest that child authors use different *types* of physical force as an option to help them resolve certain difficulties that their story characters face, thus satisfying their primitive 'instinct[s]…to hit, shove, push, and yell' (Browning, n.d.: 2) – think *pillow/foam fights!*

Lower Key stage 2

- Suggest that child authors set a story in the snowy French Alps. In an effort to get away from a persistent secret admirer or a camera crew, invite child authors to describe how their attractive/famous story character takes advantage of wax to reduce friction as they use physical force to quickly ski/sledge/snowboard down the nursery slopes and away from their undesired attention! To stimulate this writing visit http://tinyurl.com/nrz64jb for some incredible skiing clips from the *James Bond* films.

- Get child authors to write a frantic story scene for a 'search-and-find' tale in which their protagonist has to use physical force in the form of compression to hide/reduce/break down special objects or valuable items that are being desperately sought by the antagonist in the tale. Examples might include unique foods, diamonds or eternal life pills: *'Why does the antagonist want these so badly?'*

Upper Key stage 2

- Provide child authors with different kinds of magnets to gain first-hand experience of magnetism. Introduce child authors to the deceased superhero *Magnetic Kid* (see http://tinyurl.com/pwqxua7). Invite them to bring him back to life as *Magnetic Man*, exploring how he tries to cope with adjusting to modern-day life as he uses his magnetic powers to defeat different villains (see http://tinyurl.com/qxmyaqd for suggestions on how to create a supervillain).
- Child authors could be encouraged to use a literal force – *The Force* (the police) – in their story writing to help address the conflict caused by gang culture, for example. Consider the important role that buoyancy and drag play in helping the police to catch lead gang members using tracking hot-air balloons and whizzy jet-pack parachutes. *Perhaps protagonists could become Special Constables so that they are more involved in the exciting 'chase and capture'?*

Gold star!

It is important that child authors develop their independence when engaging in story writing activity (see Rumseya and Ballarda, 1985). While professionals can offer them support when needed, there are tangible story writing resources available to supplement this support. Recommended sources include *Story Sparkers* (for ages 6+) and *Writer's Block* (for ages 8+), both of which are available from *Amazon.co.uk*. Also see the *Writing* resources (Primary) available from TTS Group and http://tinyurl.com/k2efgzp.

Competitiveness!

An interesting way that story characters can resolve external conflict with others is through the use of competitions (see Bodenhafer, 1930). Opportunities for them to go head-to-head with 'the problem' (be it another person/animal/monster/machine/a force of nature/society/institution/abstract idea) allow child authors to build some exciting tension in their story writing. *Who is going to win? Who will be defeated?* (think *competitive sports, reality TV shows* and the *Top 40 music industry*). The only way that readers (and writers) will find out who is victorious is to keep on reading (or writing)!

Lower Key stage 2

- Offer child authors the story title 'The Battle of the Baubles'. Suggest that they try writing a competitive story in which two neighbours try to outdo each other by decorating the exterior of their house in the most 'extravagant' (ugly) way for the festive season. Encourage child authors to view online images of Christmas decorated houses to support their 'outrageous' descriptions of the decor. *'How is the "showiest" house determined? By other neighbours? The local newspaper? An online poll? How do passers-by regard the houses? With distain or admiration?'*
- Introduce child authors to *Competitive Golden-Ager*, a 'child-like' pensioner who *has* to be *first* in the queue for the bus, *has* to knit the *fastest* and *has* to 'slurp up all her soup' the *quickest*. *'What happens when her friend, 'Got-2-Win' Grandma, comes to visit?'* Get child authors to write a comical story about how this visitor manages to outshine the host and how this affects their relationship.

Upper Key stage 2

- Invite child authors to write an exciting story involving two small sports teams – think *football*, *rounders* or *lacrosse*. Thought shower ways in which one of the teams – the aggressive rival team – try to sabotage the other team's chances of winning e.g. *putting itching powder in players' shorts*, *using Frisbee-curving balls* or *loosening studs in boots*, and how the other team persevere with determination, discipline and a positive mind-set to eventually win.
- Verhoeff (1997: 5) suggests that 'it is necessary to incorporate competition into education to help children get used to it in later life'. Get child authors to write a '+10 years' story involving competition in some aspect of their 'later life' e.g. *getting a decent job*, *winning the hand of a girl/boy* or *being triumphant at the local quiz*. Encourage them to explore different ways that they try to cope when they are unsuccessful e.g. *cry*, *laugh it off*, *talk to someone* or *retain a positive mind-set*. For writing support, get child authors to watch interviews post-high profile games/races (think *Wimbledon*, *football matches*, *Formula One races*) in which the winners and losers are interviewed.

Gold star!

Cairney (2011) reports on the practice of teachers at Ainslie School who, as part of an annual writing festival, created 'stories in a box', carefully selecting 'connected' objects to stimulate language. Visit http://tinyurl.com/oyse7yv to find out more about the boxes and the benefits of using/adapting this teaching strategy to stimulate child authors' story writing. Alternatively, see http://tinyurl.com/pbwkbpz.

Oh, I give in!

Peha (2003a: 17) asserts that '[f]iction is all about how your character gets or does not get what he or she wants'. The song 'You Can't Always Get What You Want' by the Rolling Stones honestly reflects 'real life'; while this it is disappointing, recognition and acceptance of this is all part of growing up to be a balanced human being. Professionals may question whether it is appropriate to advocate the notion of characters 'giving up', but they are reminded that it is just a story *option* and one which child authors *may* wish to use to bring some kind of resolution near the end of their written story.

Lower Key stage 2

- Get child authors to generate a list of jobs that they cannot imagine themselves ever doing e.g. *astronaut, water slide tester, supermodel, chocolate taster* or *pop star*. Invite them to write a 'giving up' story in which story characters apply/tryout for one of these jobs/roles – '*What do they have to do at different stages of the application/test?*' – but eventually give up because they do not believe they can get the job. '*What is the moral of the story? "Believe in yourself"?*'
- There are times when we give up even before we start. Encourage child authors to write a 'effortless' story about a character who wants to do/get/see/earn/play/sing/be something but gives up on the idea before initiating anything towards it out of fear, spite or a lack of energy/time/effort/encouragement from others. Support child authors in recording the inner dialogue of characters as part of the story as they think about what they are eventually *not* going to do. '*Do they regret this course of (in)action later on?*'

Upper Key stage 2

- Offer child authors a large white flag made out of fabric or paper. Invite them to write on the flag a story which describes conflict between individuals, gangs, teams or countries, be it in the form of a game, a fight, a competition or a war. Ensure that child authors have clarity about what the conflict is over – *a person, a right* or *a possession* – offering rich descriptions of the 'clash' between the two sides. '*Eventually one "side" will have to give up and surrender. Why so? How will they do this?*'
- Introduce child authors to the idea of the *rivalrous* love *triangle* 'where the lover is competing with a rival for the love of the beloved' (Johnson, 2010: 6). In this situation one character will have to give up and back away: '*Who will that be and when do they know it is time to give up?*' Encourage child authors to carefully 'plot-plan' different ways that characters try to 'win' the object of their affection – think *chocolates, flowers, poetry* and *jewellery* – one with ultimate success and the other unfortunately without.

Gold star!

Research by Graham and Perin (2007: 5) 'found strong evidence that pupils benefited from supporting each other. Such collaborative working involved a number of processes, including: reading, planning, drafting, revising, editing their compositions, [and] checking their final copies.' Ensure that there are supported and independent opportunities for child authors you work with to engage with some or all of these processes when story writing, as appropriate. See http://tinyurl.com/paudn45 for some useful supportive information.

Avoiding one another!

Richardson (1995: 20) argues that '"avoidance" should, in some instances, be recognised as an active form of conflict resolution'. Parents/carers and professionals regularly encourage children to 'avoid getting into trouble' in an effort to promote harmony with their peers; as such, avoidance can be offered as a 'powerful weapon' (p. 24) for child authors to utilise when attempting to resolve the conflict that might be present in some of their written stories.

Lower Key stage 2

- Burns (n.d.) suggests that some people use *accommodation* as a conflict avoidance strategy – this is where the 'avoidant person win[s] favour with the [individual] with whom they are in conflict'. Get child authors to write a sensitive story where astronauts, deep sea divers or sailors 'accommodate...other[s] as a way to avoid pursuing direct negotiation' in these 'pressured' locations where they work. *'Who might these "others" be? Think aliens, sharks and pirates!'*
- Introduce child authors to two imaginary story characters: one who is a vile teacher and the other who is one of their pupils. Talk about how the teacher is always 'picking on' the pupil and this causes them [the pupil] to become *passive-aggressive* – this is where 'individuals find ways of behaving that intentionally annoys the other person' (Burns, n.d.). *'What does the pupil do? How does the teacher react? How about basing your ideas on things that might annoy me* [you as a professional]*?!'*

Upper Key stage 2

- Stonewalling is described by Gottman (n.d.: 2) as where one person 'tends to ignore [another person] and does not give any signs of responsiveness, which makes [the other person] even angrier'. Support child authors in writing a stonewalling story either about friends who fall out with each other on a city break, players who blame others for losing the game, or noisy neighbours, the climax of which results in characters stonewalling others. *'What happens when the friends/players/neighbours are needed in an "emergency" situation? Is all forgiven?'*

- Isenberg and Jalongo (2010) assert that conflict occurs when 'children have differences over rules, preferences for games or activities, or initiating or maintaining interactions'. Get child authors to write an extended story in which characters – think *soldiers*, *knights* or *police people* – overtly avoid sources of conflict by 'hid[ing], retreat[ing] or escap[ing]' (Cavazos, 2015). *'How do they alter their lifestyle and behaviour to avoid specific places, people or activities? Does this have the desired effect?'*

Gold star!

The DfES (2001) produced some wonderful teaching materials to support professionals in delivering the National Literacy Strategy (NLS). While the strategy is now defunct, professionals are encouraged to download the PDF at http://tinyurl.com/n6djpzu, paying particular attention to pp. 1–7 in an effort to 'lift'/adapt quick-fire ideas, strategies and tips to improve/enrich the learning and teaching of narrative writing in their classrooms. Alternatively, see http://tinyurl.com/pk6tjay for some useful adaptable information.

Let's reach a compromise!

Creffield (n.d.) argues that 'sometimes the only way to resolve a conflict is to compromise'. This can be problematic, not only for story characters but also for the child authors who write about them – one only has to read *The Day No One Played Together* (Helsley, 2011) to recognise the difficulties of reaching an agreement as a result of 'sides' making concessions. In an effort to help child authors develop the art of 'find[ing] ways of getting what they want without angering those around them' (Cunha, 2013), promote the use of compromise as one of their story writing resolutions.

Lower Key stage 2

- Set up a story about a birthday party in which story characters – be they (step) brothers or sisters – serve as *Birthday Planners*, working together to decide on the food, drink, party games and birthday cake for a celebrity (A/B/C/D/Z list) in the family. *'What compromises do they each have to make in order to get everything ready for the party on time?'*
- Renner (n.d., see http://tinyurl.com/qxlpyky) advocates seven tips on learning to compromise, examples of which include 'Let things go' and 'Share your beliefs and emotions'. Get child authors to write 'give and take' stories in which characters use one or a combination of these different strategies in an effort to compromise over mundane situations involving *whose turn it is to walk the dog, takeaway choices* or *which room to decorate in the house first.*

Upper Key stage 2

- Get child authors to create a list of household chores that they have to undertake to earn pocket money at home. Use this as a reference point for a written story about compromise in which story characters compromise duties with their parents/carers in exchange for other benefits such as space, social activities, resource lending and 'family time'.

- Offer child authors the story title 'My Way or No Way!'. Get them to explore the 'potential to educate' though a story that has been written by an agony aunt/uncle which sees an uncompromising character in different situations – think *playground games*, *lunch time snack trades* and *conflicts between best friends* – and who becoming very lonely as a result of their behaviour. *'How do they learn that* win–win *is better than* win–lose?'

Gold star!

There are times when professionals need access to a wealth of *additional* practical resources/strategies/ideas that they can pick and choose from (see 'Story writing "pick and mix" 1–10' for starters which can be found at the end of each chapter!). Visit http://tinyurl.com/c4ta6w, selecting from the *102 Resources for Fiction Writing* that you can adapt and incorporate into your practice in response to the 'narrative needs' of the child authors you have the good fortune of working with.

Let's talk it out!

Evans (2011: 3) advocates professionals supporting children in 'talking through a problem and agreeing on a solution' to effectively deal with conflict that they experience with others. By engaging in this important activity child authors can use this as a valuable strategy to resolve the problems that characters have in their written stories; this also gives many of them the opportunity to develop and hone their abilities of devising and recording 'spoken words' (dialogue) in written form as part of their story writing (Strauss, 2010: 94).

Lower Key stage 2

- Mirrors are famously associated with the stories *Through the Looking Glass and What Alice Found There* (Carroll, 2009) and *Snow White* (Pullman, 2012). Encourage child authors to 'merge into the story mix' a mirror which is used as a 'talking tool' for protagonists to practise with prior to them verbally engaging with antagonists to discuss situations relating to theft, cheating, lying and dishonour. Other talking tools child authors might consider include a wall (think *Shirley Valentine*), a photograph, a dog or a teddy bear.

- KidsHealth in the Classroom (2006: 3) describes *Conflict Corner* as 'a weekly radio show where people call in with conflicts that they're having and the hosts of the show help them solve their problems'. Get child authors to write a radio story based on the conflict described by Katie, Ryan, Luke or Hannah (see http://tinyurl.com/l6xyuxc, p. 5), considering the conversation they have with them 'on air'. Offer a post-script to inform readers of the outcome of their eventual *tête-à-tête*. '*What happened following the advice being given? Did it all work out?*'

Upper Key stage 2

- Buck (2011) asserts that 'every child wants to break free of their parents' [or carers'] hold, going out into the world to discover, explore and learn'. As this can be a real source of conflict between parent/carer and child, invite child authors to write a story where parents/carers and children come together to talk – *at home? On a park bench? In McDonald's?* – about them [children] wanting to, for example, go shopping with friends, attend a gig (concert) unsupervised or stay up until 9 pm. '*What are their parents'/carer's concerns and how is a compromise eventually reached?*'
- The DfES (2005: 55) suggests that professionals should '[s]peak quietly, calmly and assertively' when dealing with confrontation. Support child authors in enriching descriptions of story characters' speech – think *tone, intonation, expression, pace, fluency, phrasing, pitch* and *inflictions* – when writing about the discussions held about conflict that stems from cyber-bullying, sports, gossiping or untidiness that occurs in a futuristic story.

Gold star!

It is recognised that there are many genres of stories for child authors to read and write (see Haloin *et al.*, 2005). As contemporary twenty-first-century authors and professionals, broaden child authors' appreciation of unusual story genres (seek suitable examples from http://tinyurl.com/okpo8rs and http://tinyurl.com/78nv97t) by encouraging them to write unusual stories! Personal favourites include *Musical* (apt for LKS2) and *Twitterfic* (apt for UKS2).

Problems seeking solutions!

Cairney (2009) identifies problem solving as one of the key themes in children's literature due to the fact that 'many children love to solve problems'. He argues that there are many forms of problem solving which authors can capitalise on, and this Idea explores some of those proposed that child authors could use in their own story writing to ensure their tale has a much needed 'complication' (Cleaver, 2006: 18) to stop it from 'sagging in the middle'.

Lower Key stage 2

- The MPS (2011: 1) recognises that 'we all make mistakes [but w]hat is important is that you know how to respond to mistakes in the correct way'. Get child authors to think of mistakes they have made – *pressing the wrong button on a machine, not listening properly, failing to pass a phone message* or *speaking before thinking* – and what they did to rectify the situation. Use this as the basis for a story set in a chocolate spaceship, a dilapidated mysterious hall or at a boring toy seminar.

- Get child authors to choose a team sport that they like to play. Suggest that they write a sports-themed story in which the star player (could it be them?) is injured (accidentally/on purpose). *'How does the star player manage to contribute to the game, ensuring that the team eventually win? Think advice, guidance, prayer and verbal encouragement!'* See Tocher (2015) for practical advice on writing sports stories that could be shared with child authors as part of your taught input.

Upper Key stage 2

- Lansky (2015) asserts that too many stories, particularly the Grimms' fairy tales, 'portray girls as beautiful but helpless wimps'. Challenge child authors to write a role-reversal *girls-to-the-rescue* story in which the protagonist (a girl who is strong, capable and fearless) save the frightened boys from caves, space, monsters, wells, pirates, rabid dogs, the sea or attacking lockers in an effort to show off their 'girl power'!
- Mohr (1993: 343) states that '[a]lthough learning to work together to solve problems can at first be distasteful, willing and unwilling participants gradually realise the value of working with others and gain strength, camaraderie, and direction in the process'. Encourage child authors to use this to support their structuring of a mini-mystery story which sees story characters solving mathematical puzzles/riddles/brainteasers that unlock clues to help them find the missing cello/pufferfish/wedding dress (think *The Da Vinci Code*). See http://tinyurl.com/lwkrwnb for practical teaching ideas on writing mini-mysteries.

Gold star!

StoryJumper is a wonderful website which allows child authors to create their own story books with support that can be published online and as an actual book. Visit the site (http://tinyurl.com/yek8v78), paying particular attention to the *StoryStarter – Tell a story in 7 steps* webpage (http://tinyurl.com/oxnv2nf) which offers a wealth of smashing story ideas to supplement those offered by child authors and professionals.

Story writing 'pick and mix' 5

Here is a fifth collection of stimulating story writing ideas to engage child authors and enrich professional practices. As explained in 'Story writing "pick and mix" 1' (see pp. 20–21) this assortment of ideas is not attributed to a particular age phase but is offered more as a selection of suggestions for professionals to choose from and adapt in response to the writing needs of their learners – *put an 'X' by any that you think you might try out!*

X

Story challenges: Suggest child authors take part in class / Key stage / whole school story writing challenges! Examples that have been adapted from Foster (2014: 109) include the following.

1. Imagine you had a talking pair of shoes. Write a story about them without using the word 'the'.
2. You find what you think is a marble in your pocket. You hear a tapping from inside it and, as you examine it, a tiny creature begins to emerge. What happens next?
3. Write a story in 99 words which begins with 'Suddenly I saw...'

Story gems: The Gem was a story paper which was published between 1907–1939. It predominately featured the activities of boys at the fictional school of St Jim's. Encourage child authors to 'start up' the paper again by contributing their written stories for a notional relaunch edition.

Story sacks: Story sacks are described by the National Literacy Trust (n.d.b: 1) as 'a large cloth bag containing a favourite children's book with supporting materials to stimulate language activities and make reading a memorable and enjoyable experience' (see http://tinyurl.com/jwmpb8l for further details). But what if child authors in KS2 had the opportunity to collaborate together to create a new story book for a new story sack along with all of the supporting materials such as board games, TopTrump cards, word searches and word puzzles...?

Story bonanza: Encourage child authors to write stories for a Story Bonanza stall at the school's Christmas / summer fête, selling tales that have been written for potential buyers who attend the event e.g. parents / carers, friends and siblings.

Story beliefs: Encourage child authors to read Morpurgo's (2009) I Believe in Unicorns, adapting the title as the stimulus for their own short-story version of a longer, more substantial tale e.g. I Believe in Talking Mirrors; I Believe in Toilet Snakes; I Believe in Musical Grass.

Story writing book: In collaboration with colleagues discuss the content of Schaum's Quick Guide to Writing Great Short Stories (Lucke, 1999) at a team / staff meeting, considering its value in developing planning, improving provision, and enriching learning and teaching practices in the writing classroom.

Chapter 6

All's well that ends well!

Take my advice!

Peha (2003b: 91) argues that while there are not many types of story endings, the first of the 16 that he identifies is '[e]nding with some advice'. He asserts that 'it makes for a good ending...tell[ing] other humans what we think they should do' (p. 91). In an effort to thus help readers learn from the experiences of story characters, encourage child authors to end their stimulating stories with some supportive recommendations; after all, 'endings are about change' (Rinzler, 2011) and there is no way better to achieve this than by (potentially) changing the life of those who actually read the story!

Lower Key stage 2

- Introduce child authors to an imaginary dog with the most ENORMOUS 'sucking' snore; when he breathes in the dog draws towards him everything around where he rests! Challenge child authors to write a funny story in which story characters are sucked up into the dog's nose and are subsequently sneezed out in a different setting (think the film *Honey, I Shrunk the Kids*)! *'Where do they end up? How do they get back home? How do they eventually control the dog's snore?'* Offer some practical advice for all who snore (fathers especially) e.g. *lie on your side, go on a diet* or *go to the doctors!*
- Get child authors to identify situations where they become shy, slightly anxious or lacking in confidence. Encourage them to use these as the basis of a 'confidence story' about characters who 'lose out' as a result of their social anxiety e.g. *they miss out on the beauty pageant, being picked to go on TV* or *they are not included on the school photo*. *'Might it be useful to advise readers to be brave, believe in themselves and act confident at the end of the narrative?'*

Upper Key stage 2

- Offer each child author a coin (real/toy/self-made). Get them to throw it into a *Writing Wishing Well* (model/real) that is set up in the middle of the classroom. Ensure that they do not tell anyone what their wish was; the *only* way that this wish can come true is for it to be used as the build-up for a story which is fraught with multiple dilemmas for the protagonists (relate this to the folktale of *The*

Three Wishes). Suggest that they advise readers at the end of the written story to always be *very* careful what they wish for!

- Present child authors with the following story advice endings: *Make sure you never walk down the street backwards in your pants! Always ask who is at the back door before opening it! Do your homework as soon as you get home straight from school! Listen to Mum when she is telling you off!* Invite child authors to 'start with the end and end at the start' in terms of planning an advisory story located in a domestic setting with the final sentence serving as the starting point!

Gold star!

One way that child authors can learn to 'write well' is through the advice given by literary agents (Sambuchino, 2013). Visit http://tinyurl.com/kv7p6rz, sharing age-appropriate snippets of feedback or adapted advice to help child authors improve aspects of their story writing. Personal favourites include avoiding 'endless "laundry list" character descriptions' and 'feeling cheated [by] the protagonist waking up'. Alternatively, see http://tinyurl.com/lwmq2v4 or http://tinyurl.com/kfjbttf for information and ideas.

Lessons learned!

All writing has a purpose, be it to inform, educate, entertain or persuade. When writing stories, Johns (2004) guards against writers simply 'telling the story of what happened. Readers usually want to know what [was] learned' *as a result* of what occurred. Professionals will recognise that there are many fables and fairy tales that end with a moral or a 'lesson learned'; *The Boy Who Cried Wolf* serves as a classic example. Help child authors to strengthen their story endings by teaching their characters (and readers) some valuable life lessons.

Lower Key stage 2

- Research by Marylebone Cricket Club and *Chance to Shine* (2014: 1) found that 'over eight out of 10 (84%) of 1,000 children aged eight–16 agree[d] that experiencing winning and losing [in relation to school sport] is important'. Encourage child authors to write story about a sports day in which different rival characters compete in different events. Which 'lesson' will child authors use to influence their story e.g. *You win some, you lose some?; Never, ever, ever give up?; There's no 'I' in 'team'?*
- Becker (2014) suggests that some of the most important lessons about life can be learned by watching children. Support child authors in observing their peers / family members so that they can write a story 'based-on-seen-experiences' about the importance of friendship over possessions, how we are treated depends on the way that we treat others, and how honesty is the best policy. Ensure that there is a moral or a 'message' given at the end of the story – see http://tinyurl.com/m8g7vxq.

Upper Key stage 2

- Direct child authors to the weblink http://tinyurl.com/2afj6nb which offers both traditional and modern versions of Aesop's fables. Challenge them to write their own contemporary retelling of a selected fable using up-to-date references to popular culture and new dictionary words e.g. *bestie*, *scissor-kick* and *wackadoodle*. Emphasise the 'lesson learned' through character dialogue or an epilogue at the end of the retelling.

- Select an appropriate story from those offered at http://tinyurl.com/6pxd68g, ensuring that the 'moral box' is not revealed on the IWB. *Can child authors guess what the moral of the story is?* Offer them a selection of adapted/appropriate 'Life Lessons' (see Ngo, 2014) which can be individually presented on card, supporting them in writing a short story to exemplify their chosen life lesson *but not explicitly stating it*. Mix up the completed short stories and the 'Life Lesson' cards, challenging child authors to work together to try and match a story with the correct life lesson.

Gold star!

The brilliant *Toy Story* trilogy (Disney Pixar) serves as a wonderful stimulus for helping child authors to learn valuable 'lessons'. Indeed, the Oh My Disney (2013) blog *What We Learned From Toy Story* suggests that the toys have 'a lot of wisdom to impart, inspirational, practical, and otherwise'. See http://tinyurl.com/osw3apg for 20 'lessons' which child authors could use/adapt for the benefit of their own story writing with support from professionals. Watch video clips from the different films to help child authors understand the 'lessons' through a 'seeing-is-believing' approach.

A time to reflect

Peha (2003b: 97) asserts that:

> Often, when we find ourselves at the end of something, we want to make a judgment about it. We look back over the entire experience and ask ourselves: Was it good? Was it bad? How did things turn out for me? What's the bottom line? And then we try to sum things up as best we can.

This succinctly describes what child authors can do, with support, if they wish to use a reflective ending to 'tie up' their stimulating story. Brownhill (2014: 133) identifies a wealth of strategies to promote reflective thought, and a selection of these serve as the 'trigger' for some reflective story endings.

Lower Key stage 2

- Offer child authors a large sheet of paper on which they can draw a 'snapshot picture' based on an almost complete story they have been writing that involves enormous dice, metallic pyramids, lethal 'popping' corks or snake-like ribbons. Suggest that child authors reflect on the drawn scene, considering how story characters feel when faced with these different difficulties (see http://tinyurl.com/m9kn66x and http://tinyurl.com/72dc4tj) and how they feel now. Offer these thoughts by way of bringing their story to a reflective conclusion.

- For homework get child authors to write a story about an everyday object that overnight becomes magically 'combined' with another in their pocket, purse/wallet or bag e.g. *a key and a comb become a keycomb!* Encourage child authors to swap their stories and let their peers read and rewrite the ending of *their peer's story* by reflecting on the effects of this new 'object combo' on the discoverer and the lives of those who use it e.g. *Does it bring people fame, fortune and happiness? Are people helped or hindered by this new object?*

Upper Key stage 2

- Offer child authors extracts from different diaries – think *The Diary of a Killer Cat* (Fine, 2009), *Diary of a Wimpy Kid* (Kinney, 2007) or *The Diary of a Young Girl* (Frank, 2009). Get them to imagine that they are a different character from the 'told tale' who is looking back and reflecting on the events in the text. '*What would this character say about the events? What would* they *like to change in hindsight?*' Encourage them to write a 'recollection story' with an ending which is suitably reflective in thought and comment.

- Visit http://tinyurl.com/lv8v6lx for a series of reflective questions that professionals could ask child authors at the end of the school year. Invite them to write 'one final story' based on one of these questions, using pseudonyms for story characters as and where necessary. Encourage them to reflect on what they have learned from their experiences and how they feel this will influence the rest of their lives.

Gold star!

There are some real gems on the internet to support professionals in stimulating the story writing of child authors they work with. Consider the value of the following PDFs to enrich and 'transform' subject knowledge and story writing practices in your classroom:

- http://tinyurl.com/lqz76eq
- http://tinyurl.com/kjgb327
- http://tinyurl.com/nqq26tm
- http://tinyurl.com/kf7op6d

A not-so-happy ending!

It is common for children's stories to have a happy ending. However, many well-known stories do not actually have the typically Disney-fied 'contented conclusion' as many of us believe; in the original version of *The Little Mermaid* (Andersen, 2014), for example, the prince marries a different woman resulting in the title character throwing herself into the sea where her body dissolves into sea foam! Invite child authors to join the likes of the Brothers Grimm and engage in the 'lost art' of writing stories that do not close on a cheery note!

Lower Key stage 2

- Suggest that child authors write a 'local colour' story (one which vividly depicts a specific place at a certain point in time with rich descriptions) that involves themselves and their best friend. Build into the story a simple misunderstanding, the telling of a fib or a moment of jealousy which unfortunately results in the fictitious breakdown of their friendship at the end of the tale.
- Statistics suggest that there is an increase of children growing up in single-parent families (ONS, 2012). Invite child authors to write a 'broken-love' story in which their lead character unsuccessfully attempts to get their mother and father together again using slightly flawed strategies e.g. *writing love notes/texts with misspelt words* or *sending flowers and chocolates to each parent that are not liked by the recipient*. The published work of Jaqueline Wilson could serve as a useful source of inspiration for child authors in relation to this idea.

Upper Key stage 2

- The original ending of the movie *DodgeBall: A True Underdog Story* (2004) saw the Average Joe's team failing to win the championship. Get child authors to rewrite the ending of 'the book of the film' so that characters ultimately fail to defeat the protagonist (*Harry Potter*), do not make it home (*E.T. the Extra-Terrestrial*) or are never found (*Finding Nemo*). *How does this change the tone of the novelisation of their favourite film?*
- In *The Bad Beginning* (the first of the 13 *A Series of Unfortunate Events* books), Snicket (1999: 1) describes the story as having 'no happy ending [...] no happy beginning and very few happy things in the middle'. Challenge child authors to replicate Snicket's approach to storytelling by writing an extended friend-based story that is riddled with disappointment, disaster and despair for the lead characters – think *arguments and accidents!*

Gold star!

The inspiration for this idea came from viewing Saunders *et al.*'s (2009: 138) research 'onion'. Support child authors in considering the 5W[1]H cues (Jasper, 2006) – *Who? Where? What? When? Why? How?* – at the planning stage of their story writing by labelling up and jotting down ideas in concentric circles. Alternatively, use this diagram layout as a visual prompt for helping child authors to consider/remember the different story elements (refer to http://tinyurl.com/d6soj4r).

A time to remember

It is said that 'death comes to us all', irrespective of race, creed or sex. When 'the end' does come many people spend time thinking about loved ones who have passed away which can comfort them. Stories such as *Gentle Willow* (Mills, 2003) and *Michael Rosen's Sad Book* (Rosen, 2004) help child readers (and child authors themselves) to recognise and positively address varied feelings of disbelief, anger and sadness, along with love and compassion. Encourage child authors to use the notion of 'looking back' as a poignant way to bring a written story to a conclusion following a story character's passing.

Lower Key stage 2

- A unique way of remembering the dead is through their ashes being turned into a memorial diamond which is then set into a ring, a pendant or a pair of earrings. Get child authors to create a story character who wears one of these 'special' items that turns out to have magical powers: *'Who is being remembered via the diamond? What kind of magic does the diamond allow the story character to perform? How does this reflect the personality/temperament of the deceased?'* Consider using the story of *Greyfriars Bobby* as inspiration (see http://tinyurl. com/763tuta).
- Ganeri (2015) identifies a number of ways that different cultures and customs from around the world remember the dead. Invite child authors to select and read one, using it as the basis for a story which tells the tale of a protagonist embracing the customs of another culture in an effort to creatively remember the passing of a fascinating close family member or a close friend.

Upper Key stage 2

- Remembrance Sunday is described as 'the day traditionally put aside to remember all those who have given their lives for the peace and freedom we enjoy today' (see http://tinyurl.com/od88lxq). Offer child authors the outline of a poppy (see http:// tinyurl.com/o7t5346) into which child authors can write an emotive story extract as a way of remembering a fictitious service person (male/female) who died in the First or Second World War: *'What did they do in the War? What happened to them? How were they/are they remembered by their families?'*
- Monuments typically serve as a visual way of remembering those who have passed away. Invite child authors to write a story which opens with a number of story characters building a creative shrine in a garden or a park. Encourage them to slowly reveal who the shrine is for through the dialogue that is exchanged between characters as the shrine is built, ensuring that particular features of the shrine aptly reflect the deceased's personality e.g. *shiny objects (a bright temperament), colourful fabric strips (vibrant dress sense).*

Gold star!

It is strongly believed, from a personal perspective, that research should inform professional practice. With this in mind, professionals are encouraged to actively read and discuss the content of one of the research papers below, considering the implications for a mini-action research project into the learning and teaching of story writing in your classroom:

Research title	Author(s) and date	Weblink
Writing in English as an Additional Language at Key stage 2	Cameron and Besser (2004)	http://tinyurl.com/kopfc68
Creativity, uncertainty and discomfort: Teachers as writers	Cremin (2006)	http://tinyurl.com/ozqq3mv
Storytelling and Story Writing: 'Using a Different Kind of Pencil'	Campbell and Hlusek (2009)	http://tinyurl.com/l5aa8hf

Ending with a question?!

It is no secret that readers can feel let down by the ending of a story if they do not consider it to be 'good'; as such, Peha (2003b: 90) recognises story endings as being 'the hardest things to write'. One way to make story endings memorable for all the right reasons is through the use of a question, be it rhetorical (Peat, 2010a) or one that actually does require an answer! Professionals can support child authors by helping them to develop an understanding of different question types and how these can be used to stimulate the final line of their written tale!

Lower Key stage 2

- Challenge child authors to write a story about two best friends who fall out as a result of an argument e.g. *one accuses the other of being selfish, one thinks the other has stolen some sweets from them* or *one 'accidentally' forgets to attend the other's bat mitzvah.* Suggest that they offer an ending question to their 'sad' story such as *How could they make friends again?* to promote thought and purposeful conversation about practical ways to repair the damage done to their relationship.
- Offer child authors a series of ending questions e.g. *And what do you think he saw when he opened the door? It is enough to just* wish *for friends? Can you guess what Suzie said? Who on earth would think of looking for the Heart of Confidence there?* Support them in story planning *backwards* from the end of the story to the beginning, using extended comic strips, for example, in an effort to visually plan the story *in reverse*! See http://tinyurl.com/yf4ka6r for support.

Upper Key stage 2

- In the classic BBC sitcom *One Foot in the Grave* Victor Meldrew once asked the question 'Why do people always want to meet up?' Get child authors to use this as stimulation for an extended story about unwelcome visitors who come to their house/while they are on holiday and how story characters creatively try to get rid of them (not literally!). Remember to offer Victor's question at the end of their story as a rhetorical question, presenting the story under the title *Why Me...?*
- Challenge child authors to create their own question endings that actively promote critical thinking through the use of Bloom *et al.*'s (1956) taxonomy (see http://tinyurl.com/pj7a5y3). Share their completed story with peers/family members, evaluating the effectiveness of their question ending through careful observations and purposeful literary discussions – *perhaps they could write down their discussions and use these as the stimulus for a new story?*

Gold star!

Visit http://tinyurl.com/mxetyc for images of *17 Larger Than Life Giant Objects*! Get child authors to select one of these objects, considering what happened the day the object suddenly appeared in their classroom/school. Enrich their written tales by 'building up' the object's presence e.g. *'What if it could talk or move?'* Alternatively, have child authors come into the classroom to find a giant biscuit/Ferrero Rocher/My Purple Bar/Toblerone/Gummi Worm. *'Who put it there? Where did it come from? Do you think they want it back?'*

A twist-in-the-tale ending!

Singleton and Conrad (2000: 229) define a plot twist as 'a radical change in the expected direction or outcome of the plot of a novel, film, television series, comic, video game, or other work of narrative'. Many readers like to be surprised by what they read and Jeffrey Archer is personally considered to be a master of 'the surprise/shock ending' (see Archer, 2014). While professionals will rightly argue that Archer's stories are not suitable for child authors, the 'mechanics' that he and other established authors use to 'twist the tale' can be embraced by child authors to bring an element of the unexpected to the finale of their own 'twisted' stories!

Lower Key stage 2

- 'They woke up – it was all a dream' is a rather overused story twist ending, classically exemplified by *Alice's Adventures in Wonderland* (Carroll, 2008). Get child authors to write an inventive story about emotional robots, sherbet-dip streams and talking ornaments which form part of 'the dream'. However, invite child authors to 'twist' the story ending by creating a false sense of security in their writing. *Was it really a dream?* Describe how the lead character awakes but is unaware of little signs that suggest the fiction is actually reality e.g. *the robot winks* or *a figurine stretches and scratches its head!*

- A missing person or object provides a wonderful plot for a story with a twisted ending. Get child authors to write a story involving something or someone that goes missing (referred to here as 'the missing') – think *an animal*, *a friend* or *a valuable personal item*. Explore different ways 'the missing' is searched for, twisting the story ending by revealing that 'the missing' was deliberately hiding and not actually missing at all (it was where it should have been all the time) or had been 'strategically misplaced' to divert others' attention from a more important missing object/item/person/animal that has been taken!

Upper Key stage 2

- In the *Star Wars* film *The Empire Strikes Back* Darth Vader is revealed to be Anakin Skywalker, Luke Skywalker's father. While this bombshell appears part way through the movie, child authors can use 'the reveal' as an interesting twist to end one of their stories involving clowns, teachers, pilots, builders, vampires or zoo keepers – characters who encounter these individuals as part of their tale could turn out to be their long-lost biological parent or sibling.
- Encourage child authors to visit http://tinyurl.com/m5ku48t, inviting them to use the online generator to select a twist for the ending of a potential story. Follow the website's recommendations by engaging in some 'reverse plot-planning', carefully working out how their winter-based story can satisfactorily *lead up to* the twist. Write up the story, ensuring that their planning sheet is kept hidden from prying eyes!

Gold star!

An impressive professional resource is Shaw's (2008) *1001 Brilliant Writing Ideas*. Consider visiting http://tinyurl.com/myxn5y2 for a downloadable PDF of the book, complementing the immense wealth of ideas offered with those in this book and its sister volume (*Stimulating Emerging Story Writing! Inspiring children aged 3–7* – see Brownhill, 2016). For further ideas see http://tinyurl.com/mt4tg37.

Cliffhanger!

Bowkett (2010: 49) describes cliffhangers as a 'narrative device [which] ends the scene or chapter at a dramatic moment, leaving the reader wanting more'. They can, of course, be used to *end* a story although there are many who would argue that this leaves the reader (and possibly the author) 'unsatisfied'. Nevertheless, child authors of all ages should be encouraged to write with the intention of making their readers 'want more' – *the question is whether they actually succeed!*

Lower Key stage 2

- Time4Writing (2011: 1) suggests that there are *three* types of cliffhanger: *question*, *dialogue* and *descriptive scene*. Visit http://tinyurl.com/mlnp9hh, showing child authors the story extracts to exemplify each type. Encourage them to use one of these as the model for their own cliffhanger, using exclamations (*!*), ellipsis (*…*) and dramatic details (*the bitter, snow-filled wind*) to enrich the final sentence of their tale.

• Read to child authors one of Conklin's (2003) *Comprehension Cliffhanger Stories* (see http://tinyurl.com/ndrxv35 for a sample). Invite them to rework the story into a 'cliffhanger epic', altering the characters, setting, dialogue and descriptions to make it *their* fictional creation. *'How can you revise Conklin's cliffhanger so it works for* your *story? Think carefully about the choices you make about adverbs, connectives and nouns!'*

Upper Key stage 2

• Challenge child authors to generate a list of situations where story characters are most definitely 'in a crisis' e.g. *being pushed down a 30-metre well, about to crash a car into a mansion wall, being deliberately thrown out of an aeroplane* or *jumping from a burning train into the path of a killer cupboard*. Get child authors to 'back-plot' from this cliffhanger moment, considering how characters could get themselves into this frightening situation, 'forward-writing' from the story start.

• Visit http://tinyurl.com/km7ewbs, offering child authors the choice of one of the cliffhanger writing prompts. Get them to note how the author uses '*And then…*' to signal the cliffhanger. Encourage them to use this and other phrases such as *All of a sudden…! Quick as a flash…! Without warning…! Unexpectedly…! Abruptly…! Out of the blue…!* in their own stories, offering these also as a cliffhanger *opener* for child authors to use!

Gold star!

Let child authors into *your* story writing world by sharing examples of *your* story writing with them (notional/actual), giving them opportunities to learn from your efforts, be they positive or not so positive. *Can they help you to make your story better? Of course they can!* **Note:** If child authors see professionals as living authors they are more likely to aspire to be an author themselves (see Grainger, 2005; Ings, 2009)!

A possible sequel?

How many times have you asked yourself *'I wonder what happens next?'* or *'Is there another one?'* after reading a really good book? Many published authors satisfy their readers' curiosity/desire by writing sequels which typically form part of a series; this is particularly evident in children's literature – think *NERDS* and *Lucky Stars*. Develop child authors' writing abilities by 'continuing the story' which is what a 'follow up' is all about!

Lower Key stage 2

- Bayne (2015) suggests that writing a sequel can be 'easier than [writing the] original story because the characters have already been established'. Invite child authors to write an original story – think story titles such as *Monkey on Wheels!*, *The Mermaid's Cold*, *The Honey House* or *Black Blood* – which they then give to one of their peers who should read the story and then write a sequel for it, ensuring (of course) that they have the author's *permission* to write the sequel!
- A story sequel can be easily recognised if the word 'continued' appears in the title – think *The Frog Prince, Continued* (Scieszka, 1991). Suggest that child authors write a much-desired 'midquel' which fills in what happens in the 19-year gap from Harry's successful defeat of Voldemort to the day he sees off two of his children to Hogwarts (during the epilogue of the final book; Rowling, 2007) or the 2011 *Part Two* Warner Bros. film – *Harry Potter, Continued!*

Upper Key stage 2

- Refresh child authors' memory of fairy tales with reference to Russell Brand's *Trickster Tales* series. Also share with them select stories from Koran's (2014) *Cinderella's Son and Snow White's Daughter: The Untold Sequels to the Fairy Tales*, inviting child authors to select a different tale from the Brothers Grimm, Andersen or Perrault and 'sequel' this, proving that the story characters did not all live happily ever after after all!
- Many child authors will be aware of the *Star Wars* films – the original trilogy (Episodes IV, V and VI), the prequels (Episodes I, II, III) and planned sequels (VII, VIII and IX). Invite child authors to write either a prequel or a sequel to a story found in their own literacy books in an effort to develop their appreciation of backstory (prequel) or the expansion of an existing rich narrative (sequel). Sticky-tape this new story to either the top or the bottom of the page on which the original story is presented to signify what kind of story has been written. *Do readers/markers feel the prequel/sequel is better than the original?*

Gold star!

Sipe (1993: 19) asserts that known stories can be 'transformed' by writing 'parallel, deconstructed, or extended versions of the original tale, or the tale may be transformed through the illustrations.' Support child authors in understanding how published authors have achieved this by showing them printed examples from '[a]n annotated bibliography of transformations of traditional stories' (see pp. 25–26 of Sipe's article for a useful list), using these as a verbal/written model for their own story writing.

Story writing 'pick and mix' 6

Here is a sixth collection of stimulating story writing ideas to engage child authors and enrich professional practices. As explained in 'Story writing "pick and mix" 1' (see pp. 20–21) this assortment of ideas is not attributed to a particular age phase but is offered more as a selection of suggestions for professionals to choose from and adapt in response to the writing needs of their learners – *put an 'X' by any that you think you might try out!*

X

Story surfing: Invite child authors to write a story in which their protagonist can 'surf' from one famous story to another using their story surfboard, joining the tales at the most exciting part of the narrative. *How do their actions alter the remainder of the different stories written once they leave?*
Just a Story: Talk to child authors about the popular BBC radio game show *Just a Minute* (see http://tinyurl.com/d7eqgc). Use an adaptation of the title – *Just a Story* – as the inspiration for some very short story writing which must adhere to the writing rules: the children must write a short story without *hesitation, repetition* or *deviation* from a given / selected subject!
Story sample strips: Show child authors a small selection of paint sample strips, explaining their purpose when helping people to decorate. Invite them to create some *story* sample strips which offer just a snippet of a story which others could select and use to write a full 'colourful' story e.g. *The alarm failed to go off... The music got louder... The magic trick went wrong...*
'Spiky' stories: Share with child authors this small collection of alliterative feud-fuelled story titles, as inspired by the work of David Walliams: *The Bicker Boys; The Argumentative Auntie; The Quarrelsome Queen; The Squabble Sisters; The Fractious Friends.* Encourage them to write an engaging story which explores the reasoning behind the tense temperament(s) of the lead characters through frequent flashbacks to past events.
Ancient story writing: Visit http://tinyurl.com/lrfwfhr, challenging child authors to write select parts of a story set in Ancient Egypt using hieroglyphics to 'represent different objects, actions, sound or ideas' (Barrow, 2013) – think rebus stories.
Story Time: Get child authors to consider what would happen if one of the following time changes happened: • We had an extra hour per day (25 hours as opposed to 24 hours) • An hour only lasted 40 minutes as opposed to 60 minutes • The summer became the shortest season (just one day) • The weekend (typically two days) became longer than the working week (typically five days) Use one of the above as the stimulus for an interesting piece of 'timed' story writing, making reference to *Tom's Midnight Garden* (Pearce, 2008) and *Doctor Who's* time travel stories for inspiration!

Stimulating story writing provision and practice

Chapter 7

Inspired ideas!

Planning with ease!

There is a shared understanding in the story writing community that writing is 'a sequence of steps, with planning the organisation of the content [the plot] as one of these' (BBC, 2009: 3). The importance of story planning cannot be underestimated; for many child authors it can make the difference between them getting lost in a 'wealth of ideas and words' and actually completing their written story! There are numerous ways that child authors can 'plot-plan' with ease as the suggestions below suggest!

Lower Key stage 2

*   Model the use of different diagrams – *spider*, *thought shower/brainstorm*, *Mind Map* – when plot-planning with child authors as a whole group activity. Visit http://tinyurl.com/3h9bx or http://tinyurl.com/k26v9cz for an impressive array of graphic organisers which can be used and adapted to help child authors plan their own historical story plots – think *battles, fair maidens* and *cold castles* aka *Game of Thrones*!
*   Timelines not only help child authors to plan their story in a chronological order, but also help to assure logical sequencing and coherency. Timelines can run horizontally or vertically across the page and can combine numbers, words and pictures. Encourage child authors to write silly story (see http://tinyurl.com/pqzwe2p) timeline entries on small pieces of paper/sticky labels so that information can easily be rearranged if/when necessary; alternatively, child-friendly ICT applications can be utilised (see http://tinyurl.com/qf2xxn2 as an example).

Upper Key stage 2

*   Fold coloured paper up to create a number of box 'compartments' (between four and eight – the number will determine the length of the story). Encourage child authors to use these to plot the paragraphs that will make up their story. Suggest that they use individual paragraphs to help address key aspects of the 'fundamental pattern to narrative' (Corbett, 2003: 10) in relation to their expedition story involving cowboys/girls e.g. *opening, build-up, problem, resolution* and *ending*.

- Flowcharts may be simple (arrows linking several sequential boxes) or complicated in construction in response to the story being told (*sub-plots, alternative endings* – see http://tinyurl.com/n4x6rq6). Different shapes can be used in the flowchart to link characters, dialogue and plot points (see http://tinyurl.com/cu433cy). Offer child authors whiteboards, dry-wipe pens and erasers to help them use these outline devices to write stories about glamping, guest houses or stilts/unicycles! For professional stimulation see http://tinyurl.com/kfpxjzr for examples of adventure stories that have been created using flowcharts.

Gold star!

Many busy professionals rely on the internet to find resources/ideas to support/enrich their taught delivery and understanding. Recommended quality sites linked to story planning include:

LKS2:	*Primary Resources – English: Planning and Writing Frames*: see http://tinyurl.com/nhv5wks
UKS2:	*Teaching Ideas – Writing Fiction*: see http://tinyurl.com/85a3up9

Consider the value of embracing/adapting select suggestions to support child authors in their story planning efforts.

Think of a theme!

Martin (2011) highlights that there is a difference between *theme* and *thematic category*:

Item	Explanation	Example(s)
Thematic category	Universal experiences that every child could relate to	Friendship, Growing up, Sharing
Theme	Expression of what the author is trying to say *about* a thematic category	Friendship: 'A child can find friendship when she learns to give it'

In essence, '[t]he fully expressed theme tells us what the story is about on a philosophical level. It reflects a philosophy of the author' (ibid.). The Ideas offered below are designed to support child authors in developing an understanding of thematic categories and themes and how they can positively influence and enrich their story writing.

Lower Key stage 2

- *School:* Stott (1994) argues that the best authors choose significant events to write about, arranging them into meaningful patterns. One such pattern is 'helping others…and they will help you' – see Dewan (n.d.a) for other characteristic patterns. Challenge child authors to write a story about a pupil and their class teacher, and how situations in class call on them [the pupil] to 'help out' their teacher e.g. *collecting the register, distributing the pencils* or *tidying the book corner*. Emphasise the point that we *all* need help, no matter who we are.

- *Friendship:* Invite child authors to talk about the things that they like to do with their best friend. Get them to write a 'story sample' of when this friendship is tested – think *jealousy over spelling scores, a lie that has been told* or *money / sweets that have been taken*. Give the sample to another child author who should use it as the basis for writing a full (rich) story: *'How do story characters eventually get to understand the meaning of true friendship?'*

Upper Key stage 2

- *Winners and losers:* Read extracts from *I Am Not a Loser* (Smith, 2012). Encourage child authors to think about winning/losing situations e.g. *playing sports* or *taking part in board games or competitions*. Get them to write a POV story which looks at a situation from both the winner's and loser's perspectives, weaving these together on the page using different coloured pens or **bold**/*italic* fonts. Also, support child authors in writing about a 'win–win' situation where individuals / teams work together for the benefit of each other.

- *Courage:* Invite child authors to thought shower on strips of paper occasions when they have had to be courageous – think *standing up to a bully, moving away to another country, performing on stage* or *asking a girl / boy out*. Randomly offer these paper strips to different child authors, getting them to write a story of courage based on their given occasion that is subsequently read and critiqued by a peer. *How courageous was the protagonist? How courageous was the child author in select aspects of their story writing e.g. word choices or use of complex sentences?*

Gold star!

Display resources can be a powerful way to support child authors' story writing. Visit http://tinyurl.com/m4tbbvq, *browsing* through the *Writing* resources for *KS2* for useful ideas. Personal favourites include the *Story Writer's Tool Box Display Pack* (apt for LKS2) and the *Key stage 2 Bomb Writing Prompts* (apt for UKS2). Also visit http://tinyurl.com/o7jgphc for a wealth of downloadable story writing prompts and aids for use in the classroom in the form of posters, cards, mats, dice, signs and banners. Embrace these as valuable strategies for your own story writing display provision in the classroom.

Tinkering with tales!

As a child, personal enjoyment was sought from writing stories that were based on those already known. The ability to 'tinker' with aspects of these tales, such as adapting characters' names, locations and dialogue, allowed 'my work' to be created. Corbett (2008a: 2) refers to this as *innovation*, the second step of the storymaking process, and is a practice used by many storytellers such as Dargin (1996). Encourage child authors to write stimulating stories by *innovating* known tales with a range of what are personally regarded as 'tinkering tools', as advocated by Corbett.

Lower Key stage 2 – Tinkering Tool: Alterations

- Work with child authors to make alterations to the main characters of their known story, changing aspects of their personality, behaviour or mannerisms that directly affect the story e.g. *Billy the Bird* (King-Smith, 2013) uses his ability to fly to swoop down and steal sweets on display at the local market: *'Does he give them to hungry poor children or does he scoff them all himself? How might friends and family react to these different behaviours?'*
- Challenge child authors to alter settings in their known story 'so that a character journeys through a [run-down] housing estate rather than a forest' (Corbett, 2008b: 4). Within the context of *Hansel and Gretel* this would offer an interesting modern-day retelling of a Brothers Grimm classic, especially if child authors made reference to burnt-out cars, boarded-up windows or walls covered in colourful graffiti. See Browne (2011) and French (1995) for alternative versions of traditional tales which professionals/child authors may find useful for reference.

Upper Key stage 2 – Tinkering Tool: Change of viewpoint and time

- Encourage child authors to retell their known story from a different character's POV, relating this to how authors have developed characters in what pupils have read e.g. the arrival of Violet into Jasmine's life in the story *Midnight* (Wilson, 2008). This could be retold in a different form (text-type) e.g. a letter, a diary entry, or an email that forms part of the telling of the story.
- Support child authors in retelling their known story by retaining the story plot but tweaking with the period in which the story takes place e.g. in prehistoric/Victorian/war/futuristic/modern-day times – think setting *Storm Runners* (Mitchelhill, 2007) in the 'Roaring Twenties' (1920s). Consider relating the period to that which child authors are studying as part of their history work. Further adaptations to time include the duration (timeframe) and the season(s) in which the story takes place.

Gold star!

Engage reluctant male child authors by offering them interesting resources to write their stories with/on e.g. those used by *cavemen* (sticks in wet clay slabs), *medieval monks* (quills on parchment), *Egyptians* (bamboo reed pens on made papyrus) and *astronauts* (pencils on NASA headed paper). Consider stimulating the writing environment as well with relevant background music, costumes and 'levels' at which male child authors can write at e.g. *on the floor, on the wall, upside down* (lying on their back, writing upwards on a clipboard with pencils) or *on raised stands*. Also see http://tinyurl.com/k993yzz for research into stimulating children's imaginative writing using a virtual reality environment.

Plenty of prompts!

Unless children are natural child authors their mind is likely to 'draw a blank' when faced with a piece of paper/computer screen that they have to fill with a story. The use of prompts to kick-start and support the writing process has been the subject of interesting research (Graves *et al.*, 1994) with numerous published authors using them, along with exercise, sleep and cold showers, to help break through their dreaded 'writer's block' (Smith, 1982). The suggestions below cover a range of different types of prompts (<u>underlined</u>) to help child authors fill that page/screen!

Lower Key stage 2

- It is said that a picture says a thousand words. Offer child authors <u>photographs</u> (from home/the internet/purchased) as visual prompts for their story writing. Visit http://tinyurl.com/2anms89 for 50 stimulating images that are each accompanied with a written prompt. Alternatives include *pictures, paintings, drawings/doodles, illustrations* and *sketches*. Moving images serve as a valuable variation on static images e.g. *videos, cartoons* and *films* (see BFI, 2006).
- For those professionals who subscribe to the left brain/right brain theory, visit http://tinyurl.com/cx9jljy for some fascinating writing prompts specifically for the right and left sides of the brain to 'inspir[e] students to be recklessly creative when beginning new writing'. Use these to stimulate stories about mud kitchens, confidence boosters or the day a story character was immortalised on a stamp!

Upper Key stage 2

- Mattice (2010) reported that until recently 'All Souls College (a division of renowned Oxford University) included a one-word writing prompt essay (which was always a noun) as part of an entrance exam that [became] known as the hardest exam in the world'. Challenge child authors to write 'The Hardest Story in the World' by offering them a single <u>word</u> e.g. *Happiness, Water, Time, Sleep, Trinkets, Bullies* or *Song.* Offer two or three words to start with to initially build up child authors' confidence e.g. *Hot sun* or *Witches flying west.*
- Visit http://tinyurl.com/qxhs2ql for age-appropriate prompts in the form of <u>snapshot summaries</u> e.g. *Your character is a writer. But his new neighbours are so noisy that he can neither work nor sleep. He decides to take action...* Alternatives include offering them story <u>titles</u> as prompts e.g. *My life as a cartoonist.* An interesting prompt comes in the form of '*The elements*' (Creative Writing Now, 2013) where child authors are encouraged to '[c]hoose a set of three elements and write a story that contains all three of them [e.g. a] stolen ring, fear of spiders, and a sinister stranger'. Get child authors to write stories using the above so that they can be orally told around a residential campfire.

Gold star!

Visit http://tinyurl.com/8n998ee for a child-friendly, interactive website called *Story Starters* which 'inspire[s] students to write by serving up hundreds of writing prompts in creative combinations'. There are four *Story Starter* themes child authors and professionals can choose from: *Adventure, Fantasy, Sci-Fi* and *Scrambler*; the prompts are also differentiated by age. Click on the *Teachers' Guide* for stimulating ideas on how to use the website in the classroom as a whole group/focused group/paired/individual activity.

What if...?

Painter (in Bernays and Painter, 1990: xvi) claims that '[w]riting exercises have long been a part of the learning process for new and established writers'. One such exercise is generating *What Ifs* – questions that have the potential to fuel an entire story (see *What If?* Shipton, 1999). The creative possibilities of *What Ifs* for story writing are seemingly endless – professionals only have to visit http://tinyurl.com/n5tsbhl for a 'starting point' example to see what *What Ifs* could do for the story writing of your child authors!

Lower Key stage 2

- Get child authors to individually write a story based on a class-selected *What If* e.g. *What if a man remembered one day that he had come here long ago from another planet/the bravest woman in town was thought to be a coward/we lived till we are 210 years old/you devised a unique way to catch a criminal?* (see Snyder, 2007 for more examples). Display completed stories on the IWB, reviewing examples using *What Ifs* to improve them: *'What if Sophie added more description of the setting in this paragraph?'* or *'What if Hassan used some WOW words to raise the quality of these two sentences?'* (see http://tinyurl.com/lz7zw9d).
- Visit http://tinyurl.com/y4mkz86 for an innovative *What-if Genie* generator by Van Patter. Support child authors in adapting the suggested *What If* ideas by changing nouns, verbs and adjectives to enrich their story potential e.g. *What if a doctor tracked down a castle?* could become *What if two reindeer discovered a talking chimney?* Consider using this to stimulate stories about 'Mummy Monday'/'Man Friday', floating umbrellas or silent stories!

Upper Key stage 2

- Carlson Berne (n.d.) uses *What If* questions to come up with ideas for novels. Encourage child authors to select one from the following examples to 'feed' their own little novella: *'What if you opened a fortune cookie and found a tiny map inside [...] someone who looked almost exactly like you suddenly became very famous [...] in the basement of your house, you discovered a secret passageway [...] you picked up the wrong suitcase at the airport, and inside it was the evidence from a crime?'* Get child authors to present their story in the form of a small paper book that can be sold as part of a local charity bring-and-buy sale.

- Suggest that child authors individually create a *What If* die (for a blank template see http://tinyurl.com/pqmx5wo), presenting *What Ifs* on each face e.g. *What if the sinking of Atlantis involved pirates/J.K. Rowling asked you to write a prequel to the first Harry Potter book/you washed your dog and all his hair fell out/you kissed someone and you fell into their mouth/your mobile phone turned into dust/your favourite pop star or sports player knocked on your door?* Make these dice available as writing stimuli for 'The Most Creative *What If* Story Competition' that takes places across the entire Key stage/school!

Gold star!

Defined as 'a pivotal moment in your life guided by a seemingly insignificant decision or random act of fate that changes you' (see http://tinyurl.com/k6rzk5e), invite child authors to write an *If/Then* story – *'if this happened **then** this would happen…'*. Suggest that child authors *build on* experiences in their life using *What Ifs* e.g. *What if you had received the best grades in class?* (LKS2) or *What if you had not answered your mobile phone in class when it rang?* (UKS2).

Glorious game play!

Wenner (2009) asserts that there is a 'serious need' for children to play, a sentiment well supported by professionals who work in the EYFS! For those in KS1 and KS2 it is more difficult to offer what is considered to be the most essential type of play for children – 'imaginative and rambunctious [noisy, exuberant, wild] "free play"' – due to pressures on the timetable, the demands of the curriculum and the target-driven agenda which continue to shape the practices of professionals in the primary sector. So how is it possible to combine play and story writing, particularly in KS2? The answer is *game play*!

Lower Key stage 2

- Corbett (2009: 56) considers this idea to be a 'key game in storymaking'. Get child authors to sit in a small group with each one orally offering a single word to build a collaborative story e.g. *'There…was…a…penguin…called…Boris… who…only…ate…sweets…'* Record this story on a dictation machine and play it back once it is 'complete', reflecting critically on the story. *Could child authors individually write their own 'improved' version of it?*
- Get child authors to work in groups of three or four. One child author should offer a verbal opening sentence to a story e.g. *'Carrie decided one morning to visit her Uncle Jerry.'* Other child authors should then consider what happens next using *'How about…'* e.g. *'How about Uncle Jerry does not answer the door when Carrie gets to his house?'*; *'How about Carrie breaks into the house and finds Uncle Jerry asleep on the kitchen counter?'* See how long child authors can generate *'How about'* ideas that keep the story going. Encourage them to write up the story as a retelling for others to read and enjoy.

Upper Key stage 2

- Sit child authors in a circle with the professional in the middle with a pointer stick. Play *Storymaking Roulette* by pointing to one child author who should initiate a story involving an item selected from a small box e.g. *a torch*, *a cup*, *a candle* or *a pen*. Point to another child author without warning. *Can they keep the story going without hesitation?* Get child authors to use this story as the basis for some written imitation, innovation or invention (see Corbett, 2008a).
- Challenge child authors to come up with the most 'outrageous whoppers' (lies) they can think of e.g. *they have eaten an entire house made out of salami* or *they have touched the inner core of the Earth*. Write these down on individual pieces of paper and mix them up. Ask child authors to choose a piece of paper and write an interesting story in response to the lie from the perspective of it being based on a 'true' story!

Gold star!

At the start of the educational year suggest that Literacy Co-ordinators invest a little of their budget in one of the following practical books which offers a wealth of exciting activities to stimulate storytelling, storymaking and story games for child authors of different ages:

Age group	Title (publisher, year of publication)	Author(s)
LKS2	*Show Me A Story – 40 Craft Projects and Activities to Spark Children's Storytelling* (Storey Publishing, 2012)	Emily K. Neuburger
	Descriptosaurus: Supporting Creative Writing for Ages 8–14 (Routledge, 2013)	Alison Wilcox
UKS2	*The Bumper Book of Story Telling into Writing at Key stage 2* (Clown Publishing, 2007)	Pie Corbett
	Creative Story Writing (Levels 3–6, Ages 9–14) (Guinea Pig Education, 2008)	Sally A. Jones and Amanda C. Jones

Writing in role!

In an effort to create context for children's story writing, Schneider and Jackson (2000) advocate the use of process drama. While there are many forms of this e.g. *Reader's Theatre* and *Mantle of the Expert*, this Idea will focus on *Writing in Role*. The benefits of encouraging child authors to write as a character/different person are evident in the research findings of Cremin *et al.* (2006: 273): '[I]n addition to a palpable increase in motivation and commitment, an enhanced sense of focus, flow and ease in writing was noticeable.' *So...how can this be used to stimulate child authors' story writing?* Please see overleaf!

Lower Key stage 2

- Read *Ready, Freddy! Homework Hassles* (Klein, 2004). Get child authors to write in role as *Freddy* (male child authors) or *Freddie* (female child authors). *'Oh oh! His/her teacher has set the class a story writing piece of homework in which the lead character hates doing homework!'* Get child authors to explore how Freddy/Freddie attempts to overcome this challenging piece of writing by reluctantly completing the homework in numerous creative ways!

- Invite child authors to identify their favourite celebrity (*TV/film/music/sport*). Imagine that their fame is fading and, in an effort to get back in the limelight, the celebrity has decided to write a children's story (think Henry Winkler aka *The Fonz* from the sit-com *Happy Days*). However, because they do not have the time/energy/skills they approach the child author to serve as a *ghost writer*! *'What type of story might the celebrity want to "write"? A mystery/myth/fantasy/magical/legend/adventure story? What input (if any) do they have in "writing" the story?'*

Upper Key stage 2

- Talk to child authors about what a script writer is, explaining that unlike other writers the scriptwriter's work is meant to be read aloud. Get child authors to imagine they are a 'new breed' *Author/Script Writer combo*, challenging them to write a science fiction story in which the emphasis is placed on the quality of the *dialogue* between characters during the drafting/redrafting of their creative story. See http://tinyurl.com/mnvqd3o for support.

- Work with child authors to set up a *real world* role play area e.g. *a restaurant* or *a café*. Invite them to imagine they are *poor story writers* (think J.K. Rowling pre-Harry Potter) who frequent the café to write and keep warm. Alternatively, set up a *fantasy* role play area such as a forest or a castle as visual stimuli for *successful story writers* who have been 'brought in' by Hollywood film producers to write 'the book' for the next *Shrek/Tangled/Brave/Frozen* film. See http://tinyurl.com/p8a6msh for ideas on creating different role play areas that can be used to stimulate story writing.

Gold star!

Sentence strips are a valuable resource for story building (see http://tinyurl.com/l5v5byo and Morris, 1993). 'Energise' the use of these in the classroom by coiling blank sentence strips up into *Super Story Snails* which can be used to enrich their compound story sentences (LKS2) and offer constructive feedback on their complex story sentences (UKS2). Alternatives include bending the strip into an arch to create a *Super Story Rainbow* or folding the strip back and forth on itself to create a *Super Story Zig-Zag Bridge*. Undertake a web search for activities to use with your child authors that use sentence strips in an effort to further energise their use in the classroom.

Who am I writing this for?

The research	Research by Tamburrini et al. (1984) sought to develop an understanding of children's sense of audience in their writing.
What the research found	They found that 'the vast output of writing in schools was written almost entirely for teachers [or professionals]' (p. 195).
Implications for practice	Child authors should be encouraged to write stories for a *wide range* of readers, not just for those who are going to mark it!

So, who might these 'wide range of readers' be? Suggestions include:

Lower Key stage 2	Upper Key stage 2
• Pen pals • Fictional characters • Those in the public eye e.g. *pop/film/TV/ sports stars*	• Online community • Members of the local community e.g. *the elderly, neighbours* and *the police* • Competition judges

Those who child authors come into contact with on a daily/weekly basis could also serve as interesting audiences for their story writing e.g. *child minders, breakfast/after-school providers, sports leaders, Brownie/Beavers/Cubs' leaders, music/dance teachers* and *shop owners.* More unusual audiences might include *visitors to the school, hospital patients, royalty* (think of Princess Charlotte), *invisible friends, toys* (think *Toy Story*), *pets* (see Paradise, 2007), *future generations* (putting written stories in a story time capsule that is buried in the grounds of the school), *employers of parents/carers, characters associated with yearly events* e.g. Christmas (*Father Christmas*) and Easter (*The Easter Bunny*), *authors of children's books* e.g. David Walliams (can child authors write a story that make *him* chuckle?), *future spouses, hotel guests, and those who have passed on* e.g. grandparents. Help child authors to *select* from this wealth of writing audiences for their stories by using the following strategies:

LKS2	Create a PowerPoint presentation which individually identifies different writing audiences. Scroll through the slides, stopping at one when a child author asks you to: '**STOP!**' Alternatively, create/ use a Prezi presentation which child authors view with their eyes closed: '**STOP!**'	UKS2	With reference to either a paper or electronic map of their home country or a globe of the world, get child authors to point to where (and thus by doing so, *who*) they would like to write their story for. Alternatively, use atlases, online locators or floor maps.

It is important for child authors to not only be aware of *who* they are writing their stories for but also *why* they are writing for them. It is suggested that there are three main purposes of writing stories: to *inform*, to *entertain* and to *educate* (a fourth purpose is to *persuade*). When child authors initiate work on their stories get them to consider the reason(s) for writing for their targeted audience, ensuring that this serves as a 'driving force' for the story being told; this can also act as a useful way of evaluating the quality of their story writing as child authors can ask those who read their work what they 'took' from their story once they have finished it: *What do they know now that they did not know before? Were they 'engaged' when reading the story – why / not? What might / will they do* as a result of *reading their story?* This information could also be sought in written form, as appropriate.

Gold star!

Encourage child authors to consider different ways to present their stories for their readers e.g.:

- on paper or card;
- using ICT applications e.g. simple word processing packages, PowerPoint slides, video recordings and digital images (photographs);
- as a piece of audio using a microphone or a dictation machine.

This will influence the way in which child authors' stories are received by their targeted audience e.g.:

- being physically handed to them;
- sent either using the postal system (stories written on paper or electronically burnt onto a rewritable CD);
- through electronic means (email attachments, sound files, weblinks).

Alternatively, child authors could read it out loud to their target audience by inviting them into the classroom or going and reading it to their audience elsewhere in the school / local area.

Expert advice!

As a child author I can vividly recollect being visited at my primary school by a local poet (Jan Perry) who shared her 'words of wisdom' about writing with my classmates and then wrote a limerick about 'magical' me (I still have the poem)! There are many wonderful writers and professionals who have real expertise in the field of story writing and education. This Idea celebrates the incredible 'theory and practice' of select educationalists, sharing quality ideas to develop and enrich story writing practices with your child authors.

Lower Key stage 2

- Corbett and Moses (1991: 80) advocate the use of story hats: 'Start a collection of hats. Some could be designed and made by the children.' Wear these when reading or telling stories to children. Consider getting child authors to wear these when *writing* stories. *What sorts of stories might different hats help child authors to write?* See http://tinyurl.com/mey2ao5 for an innovative *Fanciful Story Hat*!

- Malindine (2013: 8) offers the acronym NECCKS to help child authors remember how to correctly punctuate speech:

  N – New speaker, new line. E – Everything that is spoken needs speech marks. C – Capital letters start the speech. C – Commas to separate words spoken from words not spoken. K – Keep it down! Don't tell the whole story in speech. S – Speech marks at the start and end of a piece of speech.

  How well can they use this in their own written stories? Perhaps they could use different colours in their writing to indicate each aspect? Alternatively, see http://tinyurl.com/ocdshtr for a wealth of fantastic ideas for improving writing.

Upper Key stage 2

- Peat (2002: 61) argues that 'a final, important, ingredient of successful locational writing which is often neglected in pupils' writing is "the weather"'. Encourage child authors to match the emotional state of characters (a), to the weather (b), and to create atmospheric locations (c), e.g. *Delighted* (a), *Sparkling sunshine* (b), *A warm breeze danced through the well-kept gardens that were rich with fragrant, colourful flowers* (c). Further use of this could relate to the use of metaphors and similes.
- Foster (2014: 109) warns 'how "said" is often overused when [child authors] are writing dialogue and how important it is to be aware of alternatives...most of which are more expressive.' Present examples such as 'announced...babbled... cried...declared...growled...interrupted...mumbled...questioned...remarked... screamed...wailed...whispered...' on hanging mobiles, speech bubble-shaped sticky labels, washing lines or 'Said Scrolls' for use in their juicy stories that are filled with dialogue.

> ### Gold star!
>
> Haloin *et al.* (2005) have compiled a valuable grid which details characteristics associated with different genres of text. Visit http://tinyurl.com/956mbo8, considering using this as a resource to develop personal/child authors' subject knowledge (as appropriate) about story types, strengthen direct teaching points, shape assessment criteria, or positively influence story writing efforts. Older child authors could be encouraged to practise writing quick genre checklists prior to their story writing as this can help them to remember the key features/elements and develop structure and coherence in their tales.

Story writing 'pick and mix' 7

Here is a seventh collection of stimulating story writing ideas to engage child authors and enrich professional practices. As explained in 'Story writing "pick and mix" 1' (see pp. 20–21) this assortment of ideas is not attributed to a particular age phase but is offered more as a selection of suggestions for professionals to choose from and adapt in response to the writing needs of their learners – *put an 'X' by any that you think you might try out!*

X
↓

Fame story: Andy Warhol is attributed to the famous quotation *'In the future everybody will be world famous for fifteen minutes'*. Invite child authors to write about their 'claim to fame' in a story fuelled by celebrity culture and reality television e.g. *becoming a model, appearing on* The X Factor or *scoring a goal blindfolded at Wembley.*
Flush story: Get child authors to imagine that they are going on holiday abroad with their family in an aeroplane. During the flight they need to use the lavatory. Upon pressing the flush button the vacuum suction is *so* powerful that it sucks them into the toilet and out into the open sky! *What are they flying over? How do they land safely? Who/what helps them? How do they manage to be reunited with their family?* As Copeland (2000) puts it: 'The Decision Is Yours.'
Story quirks: Enrich written descriptions of characters, making them memorable for the reader (and child author) with quirky observations e.g. *He wore a watch on both arms to make sure at least half of him was on time; She was so freckly that from afar she looked as if she was permanently covered in sand; The dimples in his face made him super cute!* Encourage the use of metaphors and similes with older child authors.
Story scrap book: Purchase a large A3/A2 scrap book, encouraging child authors to collaboratively contribute to the 'building' of this as a story writing class resource. Invite them to bring in items such as *newspaper headlines, jokes, magazine pictures, notes, song lyrics, retellings of dreams, quotations, photographs, postcards, adverts* or *real objects (flat)* – *anything* which might offer others story stimulation. Alternatively visit http://tinyurl.com/mb9j6g7 for an innovative story scrapbook app.
Shaped story: Present child authors with pieces of paper that are cut into large punctuation marks/symbols as a way of helping to remind them of the focus of the tale e.g. **?** (a mystery 'who-dun-it' story), **£/$** (a 'rags-to-riches' or 'riches-to-rags' story), **+** (a 'new addition – *baby perhaps?* – to the family' story) or **−** (a story of loss). Other ideas include **…** (a cliffhanger/mystery story) and **.** (a final ending/everything is resolved/completion/non-negotiable/definitive story).
ABC story: Invite child authors to write a story in which there is at least one word which starts with a different letter of the alphabet. Variations on this idea include the following. • At least one word in the story must *end* with a different letter of the alphabet (both conventional and reverse ordering) • Write the story with the alphabet sequence guiding the word order as much as possible e.g. *Andy bought Carrie's dad every florescent golf hat in Jenny's kiosk. Larry…*

Chapter 8

Resourcing the story stimulation!

Pictures and photographs!

Open any non-fiction book for children and readers are likely to be overwhelmed with visual stimuli in the form of pictures and photographs that support the printed text. Armes (2009) asserts that these '[g]raphics are great for stimulating new [creative writing] ideas'. These graphics can come in the form of *real artwork*, *digital images*, *hand-drawn illustrations*, *reproductions*, *printed snapshots* and *postcards*. With support from professionals, child authors can use these as inspiration for their stimulating stories!

Lower Key stage 2

- It is suggested that a picture says a thousand words. Challenge child authors to write a story using an agreed-upon number of words in response to one of the photographs found at http://tinyurl.com/kgn2xlo. Use the text in the speech bubbles provided on the photographs to help 'focus the story'. Alternatively, remove these for those child authors who prefer the more open-ended image. For open-ended story *titles* see http://tinyurl.com/mdzm72q.
- Visit The National Gallery's (2015) *Take One Picture* website, exploring its creative content. Consider the value of using *The Picture* (painting) or inspiration from the *Literacy* section of the *Across the Curriculum* tab to stimulate child authors' story writing in response to famous artwork e.g. '*How did the artist celebrate the completion of his/her painting? What did they do the day after they completed the painting?*'

Upper Key stage 2

- Anstey and Bull (2009) suggest that photography is a time-efficient way for children to tell a story. Get child authors to illustrate short, morally driven story books – think *Aesop's Fables* (Jones, 2006) – that they have written for younger children in the school using staged digital photographs taken by their peers to accompany the story text. See http://tinyurl.com/o2dmhfy for some apt morals to write about.

- Encourage child authors to use their own drawings, paintings or sketches produced as part of their *Art and Design* curriculum work as stimuli for *others'* story writing. Suggest that they present their work as part of a Class Gallery, focusing on an aspect of another artist's work by using a view finder; use this to stimulate either the opening, middle or ending of their extended ghost story e.g. *'What is the significance of the lipstick in the middle of the tale?'*

Gold star!

There are many wonderful online resources and published texts available to support professionals and child authors in using pictures and photographs as prompts for story writing. Recommended materials include *The Images Shed* (see http://tinyurl.com/nq5bfxq) (apt for LKS2) and the work of Kellaher (1999) (apt for UKS2). Explore these with colleagues, considering the value of adding or adapting these materials to enhance current provision and practice. Other resources and ideas can be found at http://tinyurl.com/q53casq for lower ability KS2 child authors.

Paintings and drawings!

The J. Paul Getty Trust (n.d.) puts it beautifully when it states that:

> Works of art often tell stories. Artists can present narrative in many ways – by using a series of images representing moments in a story, or by selecting a central moment to stand for the whole story. Narrative works often illustrate well-known historical, religious, legendary, or mythic stories. Sometimes, however, artists invent their own stories, leaving the viewer to imagine the narrative.

With the support of professionals, child authors can capitalise on the creative story potential that is seemingly so richly provided by paintings and drawings!

Lower Key stage 2

- Create a 'Painting PowerPoint' which displays images of children by the likes of *Lowry, Rego, Hogarth, Thomas Gainsborough* and *Winifred Nicholson*. Get child authors to consider what could happen if a child or two 'stepped out' of their paintings due to stillness boredom and went with them [the child author] on a memorable adventure. *Where would they go? What would they see/do there? How would it be 'memorable'?* Think *performing as part of the circus, becoming a clothes designer* or *composing a Number One chart hit!*
- Read *The Drawing that Talked* (see http://tinyurl.com/phqou75). Get child authors to consider what *their* drawings might say to them when they put pencil to paper at home! Write a story in which a drawn sketch gets the child author into trouble with their parents/carers/friends/pet by *making rude comments/sounds,*

lying or *teasing others*. Alternatively, use *The Day The Crayons Quit* (Daywalt, 2013) as inspiration.

Upper Key stage 2

- Share with child authors some key facts about Aboriginal art (see http://tinyurl. com/nu74mq2). Support their understanding of the significance of symbols, colour and patterns in this art form with reference to http://tinyurl.com/n6c2u5o, challenging child authors to 'tell the tale' through a written story by interpreting selected Aboriginal artwork found in books, catalogues, portfolios, anthologies, internet-based compositions or those created by child artists in class.
- Engage child authors in a 'Drawing-Story-Peer-Loop' by getting them to write a historical story in response to a historical drawing. Give the written story to a peer (Peer 1) to read, who then creates a drawing as a visual representation of the tale. Ask Peer 1 to then give their drawing to Peer 2 who should write a story based on the drawing they have been given. Once this is complete ask Peer 2 to give their written story to the original child author. *How do the two stories compare?*

Gold star!

Huff (2000: 6) advocates the use of puppets, props and story corners to stimulate 'playful tales' through storytelling opportunities. Support child authors of all ages in making and using box/finger/folded paper/glove/hand/stick/tube puppets and story walls/aprons/waistcoats/boxes/cubes/cans/bags in an effort to 'stimulate imaginations...develop oral communication skills...[and] create a love of books, reading and, eventually, writing' (ibid). See http://tinyurl.com/ ovu3ba9 and http://tinyurl.com/npmcch7 for practical support in making story puppets, seeking online support for making, creating and using props and story corners.

Colours and shapes!

Church (2014) acknowledges 'two very noticeable attributes of the world around us': colour and shape, recognition of both which form part of all children's core learning. As there are many 'colourful' (exciting) children's stories and published compilations of shape poetry available (see Foster, 2005), child authors should be positively encouraged to utilise the creative potential that colours and shapes can offer their own story writing (with support from professionals, of course)!

Lower Key stage 2

- Extend child authors' vocabulary by 'colouring their adjectives'. Show them how to add a simple colour to a noun e.g. *a red apple*, building the 'reader's vision and the story's imagery' with either alternative colour choices e.g. *crimson, ruby* or *scarlet*, or comparison (simile) e.g. *The apples hung like balls of blood in the trees* (see Rose, 2006 for further information). Use these strategies to enrich the descriptive passages of a group/class story entitled *The Day the World Woke Up* _____ (insert colour choice here!).

- Williams (2008) asserts that 'a life well-lived is a story dying to be told'. Encourage child authors to write a story about the life of a fictional character based on the amalgamated 'lived experiences' of different family members, presenting parts of the tale on separate pieces of shaped paper (tiles) which can be arranged by the reader into an attractive story mosaic. Alternatively the paper could be shaped like jigsaw pieces, bricks (a 'story wall') or footprints to physically represent the journey – be it *physical*, *emotional* or *spiritual* – that is taken by a character through the story.

Upper Key stage 2

- Stevens and Kraneveld (2013: 1) report on how the 'AkzoNobel Decorative Paints company believes that making our surroundings more colourful has a positive effect on how people live and feel'. Challenge child authors to write an extended story about a group of volunteer painters and decorators who transform the lives of elderly people or orphans by simply adding colour to their care home/orphanage in the dead of night! *'How does this transformation affect/touch/change the lives of the elderly/orphans and those who carried out this transformation?'*
- Offer child authors different kinds of paper that are cut into various shapes, using this to enhance the story being written on it. Base these stories on one of the following 'shaped' story titles: *My Square* [boring] *Week!*; *Twister Tale!* (circular paper cut into a coil); *What a Tangled Web We Weave!*; *My Time in Prisonm!*; *Triangular Turmoil!*; or *The Ball of Doom!*

Gold star!

Colourful Stories is described as 'a visual support strategy which helps children to learn about the structure of stories and become more confident about telling and writing stories'. Created by Elks and McLachlan (2013 – see http://tinyurl.com/ppe6spf), this resource can be used by professionals and parents/carers with children in the EYFS right through to UKS2. Visit the website for more information, considering the value of utilising this as a new strategy to support different child authors and their story writing in your classroom.

Newspapers and magazines!

Research into children's reading habits suggests that 'more [girls and] young people from White backgrounds read magazines...and more [boys and] young people from Black backgrounds read...newspapers' (Clark, 2011: 5). With many child authors coming into regular contact with newspapers and magazines in a variety of different contexts – think *their home*, *the classroom* and *in the doctor's/dentist's waiting room*

– professionals should be encouraged to help child authors to see these as a 'sizzling source of potential' that can invigorate their story writing.

Lower Key stage 2

- Share with child authors interesting headlines that have been cut out of newspapers and magazines. Support them in exploring the 'story potential' by getting them to collaborate in pairs to write a story inspired by a particular title e.g. *Animals on the loose from local zoo!* could be about a newly employed keeper who accidently sets free some of the animals and tries desperately to capture them with nets, drugged darts and traps before their boss finds out!
- Energise preparations for story writing by engaging child authors in purposeful drama activity using newspapers as a stimulus. Visit http://tinyurl.com/mek8whl, reflecting on the content of the PDF in relation to using different techniques to 'get into' a newspaper story and how this work can influence/shape new and exciting tales for child authors to eventually write.

Upper Key stage 2

- Work with child authors to select a story from a newspaper or a magazine which is considered to be 'newsworthy' (see associated criteria set out by Post-News Educational Services, n.d.: 10). Encourage them to 'lift' situations/events, locations or the names of individuals for the benefit of their own story writing, enriching their narratives about mysterious marbles, dungeons or killer hamsters with the 'lived' experiences/settings/names of others.
- Select a current magazine article that is likely to be of interest to child authors – think *fashion*, *music*, *TV* or *celebrity-based*. Try to find a story that involves a number of different people e.g. *the cast of a television show* or *members of a pop band*. Get child authors to write a story for the magazine *as a fictional story* from a different POV so that readers see events with a different pair of eyes e.g. a cast/band member leaving – *how similar/different are the two stories?*

Gold star!

A valuable way to improve child authors' story writing and to develop professional practice is in response to findings and recommendations. These are likely to be influenced and shaped by government policy, research reports and literacy organisation guidance. Choose from one of the following weblinks below, considering the findings and recommendations offered, and how practical suggestions could be integrated into your existing practice:

- *http://tinyurl.com/ ormzjox*
- *http://tinyurl.com/ nm3kt58*
- *http://tinyurl.com/ nqq26tm*

Music and sounds!

DeNora (2000) asserts that music helps to create an environment which is good for concentrating and focusing – personal reflections note that this entire book was written while music was playing in the background! Disney's *Fantastia* and Prokofiev's *Peter and the Wolf* serve as two well-known examples of how music has been used to stimulate storytelling; one only has to hear the sound of a descending glissando (a rapid sliding down of the musical scale) from a slide whistle to imagine someone or something falling down or over! With support from professionals child authors can learn the true potential of music and sounds in helping to stimulate their written stories!

Lower Key stage 2

- Play child authors pieces of instrumental 'mood' music, getting them to think about the 'tranquil action' that could be going on in a story during which this background music might be played e.g. *characters taking a gentle stroll, napping, reading, reflecting, sketching* or *gardening*. Challenge them to 'turn up the action' by bringing in a new character to 'spice things up' – think *antagonistic astronauts, talking kiwis, animated ornaments* or *dippy doctors!* Get them to write their story quickly in response to the 'speedy action' as up-tempo instrumental music is played.
- A favourite game on the popular BBC Radio 4 game show *I'm Sorry I Haven't A Clue* is *Sound Effects*. Encourage child authors to give an oral reading of stories they have written, inviting peers to attentively listen while improvising appropriate sound effects with their mouths, bodies or available instruments to complement the story being told. Consider looking into the BBC's *Ten Pieces* project (see http://tinyurl.com/ouzp3tl) as further inspiration for musical-inspired story writing.

Upper Key stage 2

- Research undertaken by Appel (n.d.: 12) (an 11-year-old-boy) found that '[professionals] said that having the music didn't make any difference to the children's quality of work' when it was played as they wrote. Engage child authors in some participatory research by playing different pieces of music as they write different kinds of stories e.g. *anecdotes, chillers* and *school tales*, examining their completed work to ascertain the effects of music on the quality and quantity of their story writing for the school radio station.
- Get child authors to add a little extra spice and pizazz to their written stories e.g. *domestic tales, mysteries* and *science fiction*, by presenting them electronically using available computer software, attaching recorded sound files that they have created with peers to the story text for some engaging auditory stimulation! See http://tinyurl.com/qg6xobr for inspiration.

Gold star!

EmpoweringWriters.com advocates the 'showing rather than telling' approach when writing about the reactions of story characters in response to their feelings. As child authors build in their storytelling and writing confidence, encourage them to replace simple *tellings* – 'He was happy' – with *showings* of characters' feelings through facial and body movements e.g. 'smile on face...heart leaps... jump up and down...hands clasped together...eyes open wide'. See http://tinyurl. com/po52bnk for more examples. For less able child authors use physical body positions and actions to exemplify 'showings', referring to relevant illustrations in picture books as well.

Songs and rhymes!

It is recognised by the likes of Parlakian and Lerner (2010: 17) that song lyrics and rhymes 'tell a story'. It would be a shame if child authors were not taught about the rich potential that songs they sing along to and rhymes that they can recite have for their story writing; it is thus important that professionals not only actively *teach* children songs and rhymes as part of the curriculum but also show them how they can assist child authors in being creative and innovative story writers.

Lower Key stage 2

• Talk to child authors about the 'more sombre origins' (Evans, 2013: 8) of different nursery rhymes e.g. *Ring-a-Ring o' Roses*. Challenge them to write a historical story which integrates into the tale the 'dark meaning' of the rhyme selected. Offer these to peers or parents/carers. *Can they guess which nursery rhyme the story is based on?* See http://tinyurl.com/njtmmy2 for a useful PDF which details the historical origins of select nursery rhymes.

• Get child authors to identify their favourite pop song in the charts, inviting them to talk to others about how the lyrics/music makes them 'feel' (**not** just 'happy' or 'sad' – see http://tinyurl.com/neabxk8 for suggestions). Support them in developing a story which puts story characters in different situations where they experience the same kind of feelings. *Might their favourite song be playing in the background, perhaps?* Situations might include going to the vets, giving blood or visiting their 'pongy' old uncle.

Upper Key stage 2

• Introduce child authors to the idea of narrative poems – see http://tinyurl.com/larkpp6 for examples. Invite child authors to take one of their written stories from their literacy books and present this as a narrative poem. Alternatively, get them to take a famous narrative poem and write it up as a fictitious story – see pp. 56–58 of http://tinyurl.com/q5m6j8x for interesting information and ideas.

- Many child authors have favourite songs but they are likely to be unaware of the inspiration behind the lyrics e.g. *Ben* by Michael Jackson is all about a pet rat! Get child authors to choose their favourite song and look carefully at the lyrics, identifying a word, a choice of phrase or an image which they believe serves as the 'song spark'. Challenge them to write a fictitious 'story behind the song' which shows readers what influenced the song to be written (imaginary/real) – think *Lucy In the Sky With Diamonds* (The Beatles).

Gold star!

There is evidence to suggest that the story writing skills of child authors can be developed through the use of ICT. Select one of the stimulating readings offered below, considering the implications (notional/actual) that could be made to child authors' story writing performance through using more ICT in your classroom:

Key stage	Title	Authors	Weblink
LKS2	Collaboration, creativity and the co-construction of oral and written texts	Rojas-Drummond *et al.* (2008)	http://tinyurl.com/kwb8h68
UKS2	A 'computer tutor' to assist children develop their narrative writing skills: Conferencing with HARRY	Holdich and Chung (2003)	http://tinyurl.com/ovuyuwz

Animation and film!

The immense power of animation and film in stimulating and supporting story writing cannot be underestimated; VIA University College (2013: 2) asserts that '[u]sing animation as a tool to encourage and develop children's learning is not only fun but effective' in enriching 'skills and competencies [such as] storytelling [and] concentration'. With the potential to excite, engage and assist child authors, professionals should see animation and film as an essential pedagogical device for their story writing 'toolkit'!

Lower Key stage 2

- Watch the animated video *The Book of Butterflies by Michael Leunig* from *The Great Animations Shed* (visit http://tinyurl.com/o396flo). Invite child authors to consider other animals that could come out of the book. *What different problems might these create for the lead protagonist?* Consider writing their problem-filled story using different coloured pens/pencils to reflect the blaze of colour on the animals' skins when the book is opened.

- Paton (2014) reports on a study by Oxford University Press which found that '[w]atching films and playing computer games can have a positive impact on children's vocabulary'. Encourage child authors to thus incorporate story characters (e.g. the Minions from *Despicable Me*), objects (portals from *Monsters Inc.*) and phrases ('Everything is awesome!' from *The Lego Movie*) in tense stories about 'floods, burst river banks, power cuts and rescue operations'.

Upper Key stage 2

- Encourage child authors to watch *The Arctic Circle* animated video from *The Fantasy Shed* (visit http://tinyurl.com/kmx3uxl). Use the teaching prompts ('Writing opportunities') available to engage child authors in story writing activity, supplementing these with quizzical questions to stimulate creative thought e.g. *What other fruits could 'grow' from the tree and what effect do they have on the man? What would happen if the box befriended the man? Who is 'operating' the box?* Offer these for child authors to use as potential fuel for their rich narrative set in 'the cold', getting child authors to write their story with gloves and scarves on to reflect the chill from off the white, icy page!
- Visit http://tinyurl.com/k5pw677 for a remarkable 'teaching guide to using film and television with three- to eleven-year olds' called *Look Again!* (BFI, 2003). Focus on Chapter 2 (pp. 7–13), considering how different teaching techniques can be used to develop aspects of child authors' story writing in response to observed film segments e.g. writing extended story passages that would 'Attract [specific] Audiences' (see p. 11) when watching tween films such as *Lemony Snicket's A Series of Unfortunate Events* or *Hairspray*. Alternatively, see BFI (2006).

Gold star!

While this book aims to offer professionals a wealth of strategies, ideas and tips for the classroom it does not claim to be 'the definitive' resource for supporting story writing. Consider investing in one of the following texts to supplement your own personal bank of story writing suggestions:

LKS2	*25 Quick Mini-Lessons to Teach Narrative Writing* by Leochko (2000)	*Creative Writing for Kids: Vol 1 & 2* by Harrington (2015) (LKS2 or UKS2)
UKS2	*Adventure Stories for Ages 9–11* by Powell (2010) (one of a series of Writing Guides with a CD-ROM)	

Toys and trinkets!

Children's love of toys is universal, and it is widely recognised that toys have an important part to play in their development, largely because 'their play is often influenced by the toys they use' (TRUCE, 2009–2010: 3). Children's stories such as *Pinocchio* and *The Velveteen Rabbit*, along with family movies such as *Toy Story* and

The Christmas Toy highlight the real potential that toys have for stimulating chil authors' story writing, particularly if these toys are 'living'. This potential also applies to trinkets despite the very name suggesting 'a thing of little value'!

Lower Key stage 2

- Dewan (n.d.b) asserts that in the toy genre of stories '[s]ometimes toys come alive at night when no one sees them'. Encourage child authors to use this as a stimulating timeframe in which they can 'story plot'. Get child authors to carefully think about *how* their toys actually come to life (*struck by lightning* or *'powered' by the dark?*) and what their purpose is for living (*tidying up after their owner, doing their owner's homework* or *caring for broken toys?*). Quietly play Tchaikovsky's *Nutcracker Suite* or Leopold Mozart's *Toy Symphony* as child authors write in an effort to offer them some auditory stimulation for their 'toy story'!
- Encourage child authors to bring from home examples of promotional trinkets (mass marketed merchandise customised with company names) such as *pens, key chains, coffee mugs, fridge magnets* and *note pads*. Display these, inviting child authors to write a magical story with one of these trinkets serving as 'story fuel' e.g. *a note pad that accurately predicts the owner's future* or *a found key chain on the end of which is a small mechanism that unlocks the door to the* Kaleidoscope Dimension.

Upper Key stage 2

- This activity is an adaptation of *Letter From an Old Toy* (DfES, 2009: 6). Write 'story requests' for child authors to find inside a Second World War evacuee's suitcase (model/real) along with an old toy e.g. *I have forgotten the last time I read a story about toys that made me laugh out loud – can you write one for me?* or *What do toys talk about when their owners are not around? How about writing me a story full of dialogue to effectively convey the different toy characters?* Invite child authors to write an exciting story in response to their chosen request.
- Offer child authors the story title *The Timeworn Trinket Shop*. Explore as a class where they think the shop is located, who the shop belongs to, what different kinds of trinkets the shop sells, and who comes to buy them. Consider the 'feel' (atmosphere) of the shop and the influence that different characters have on this: *'What happens when old Mrs. Barker barges into the shop one dark and cold morning?'* Consider writing the story on 'timeworn' paper (see http://tinyurl.com/oq9qe5 for ideas!).

Gold star!

Visit http://tinyurl.com/crd4rc4 to find out all about *Story Strings*, Bowkett's (2010) wonderful story writing resource. Simple to make and use, Bowkett advocates the use of *Story Strings* in both KS1 and KS2. This idea can be easily adapted for children with additional needs by attaching items (real/images of) to a string washing line to help promote simple story sequencing e.g. *straw, sticks, paper bricks* and a *pot* for the story of *The Three Little Pigs*. Also see http://tinyurl.com/ladctj6.

Random inspiration!

Allen (2010: 36) draws a distinction between the 'Inspired Writer' and the 'Real Writer': the first 'is a figure for whom writing comes easily' whereas the second 'admit[s] to struggling with writing' (p. 35). Most child authors will fall into the second category and one of the reasons for this struggle is the need for inspiration to 'fire their desire' to put pen to paper/finger to keyboard. The ideas presented below are random in their content yet are deliberately inspirational in their drive to get child authors writing stimulating stories.

Lower Key stage 2

- I personally love thinking up children's story titles. Offer child authors the following three-word title suggestions, inviting them to choose one and take the story wherever they would like it to go: *The Tree Taker, The Reclusive Sun, The Flightless Football, The Liquid Mirror, The Butterfly Bird, The Riddled Necklace, The Bottomless Pit, The Pain Gatherer, The Temperamental Toaster, The Regale Beagle, The Mute Fairground, The Miserable Wallet* or *The Cold Fire*.
- Provide child authors with objects and collections of items (in sacks or boxes) which purposefully take them by surprise e.g. *a giant egg* (see http://tinyurl.com/psh2rle), *car engine parts, a torn letter, hairbrushes on a string loop, a snapped ruler, a message in a bottle from the head teacher, glitter-filled salt and pepper pots* or *a shredded dressing gown*. Visit http://tinyurl.com/cv73zyj, using different questions to 'spawn the seeds' of a superhero story in their minds that is subsequently transferred onto the page!

Upper Key stage 2

- Stewart (2008: 2) asserts that 'confidence and self-esteem are probably the most needed attributes in the world, but sometimes they can be the most difficult ones to build up'. Get child authors to write a 'sureness story' about an unconfident character, whose lack of belief in themselves prevents them from living different aspects of their daily life. Explore what happens when their confidence is boosted through tablets, injections, lozenges, liquids/syrups, inhalants, creams or aerosols: *'Does the boost last for long? How is the confidence of the character eventually boosted naturally?'*

- Share with child authors the idiom 'made of money'. *'What if humans were actually made of money? How would this change (!) the way we live our lives?'* Get child authors to write a sci-fi story which tells a tale of the trials and tribulations of being made out of paper and coins: *'What would you eat? What happens when it rains? How would you lose weight? How would you pay for things? What threat is posed by the evil "Debt Collector"?'*

Gold star!

Want some cracking story writing ideas? Then consider downloading the PDF available at http://tinyurl.com/mug8old, exploring the wealth of creative writing activities offered within it. Adapt these in response to the needs and capabilities of the child authors that you work with, dipping into this resource for ideas to stimulate homework, holiday tasks or writing challenges. Other suggestions and advice can be found at http://tinyurl.com/ppva4nx.

Story writing 'pick and mix' 8

Here is an eighth collection of stimulating story writing ideas to engage child authors and enrich professional practices. As explained in 'Story writing "pick and mix" 1' (see pp. 20–21) this assortment of ideas is not attributed to a particular age phase but is offered more as a selection of suggestions for professionals to choose from and adapt in response to the writing needs of their learners – *put an 'X' by any that you think you might try out!*

X

	Story homework: Drabble (2013 – see http://tinyurl.com/qekjakd) argues that: 'Some of the most popular summer homework projects involve story writing.' Click on the weblink offered above for 'plenty of resources to help your pupils become great story writers', adapting them to suit the needs and interests of your child authors. Provide parental / carer support to ensure these projects are actually undertaken!
	Story dreams: Encourage child authors to share with you their dreams / aspirations for the future – think *occupations, experiences* and *people.* Use these as the 'fuel' for a story about the reality of their 'lived' dreams in the future. *Is it everything they expected it to be? Why / why not?*
	Story book: There are many known 'books' e.g. *The Jungle Book* (Kipling, 2007), *The Book of Dragons* (Nesbit, 2012) and The Book of Life found in the Bible. Challenge child authors to write a story entitled or about 'The Book of _____' – *Cakes / Rabbits / Songs / Adventures / Smells?* Support them in presenting their story as a hardback book (see http://tinyurl.com/lg92m8c). Alternatively, child authors could write '_____ology' books in the style of the *Dragonology* or *Pirateology* series e.g. *Sweetology, Horseology* or *Twerkology!*
	Story statements: Whitaker (n.d.) identifies 'selected teaching practices that are well recognised in the profession as being effective in helping students [to] develop as writers'. Download the PDF (visit http://tinyurl.com/6t232cg), exploring how the statements validate / suggest improvements to existing writing provision and practices in your classroom / school as part of a staff / team meeting.
	Story rewards: Epstein (2014) suggests that: 'Perhaps one of the most important aspects of developing children's writing is to provide positive reinforcement for their efforts without regard to grammar and spelling errors.' Talk to child authors about the kinds of 'reinforcement' that *they* would like to receive from professionals (within reason!), be they in the form of verbal praise, stars, stamps, sweetie treats, certificates or 'special' writing resources such as scented pens, shaped rubbers or sparkly notebooks. *It's then just a case of stocking up!*
	School-wide stories: The Teacher Support Force (2011) argues that: 'When strategies for teaching writing include school-wide celebrations of children writing, magic happens and teaching the writing process becomes a community event.' Visit http://tinyurl.com/l2zrns3 for details about the *Spring Flower* [Writing] *Show,* embracing and applying the practice described to other school-wide events e.g. *One Book / World Book Day / Book Week* (stories written in response to selected books / themes), *Auctions* (of 'first edition' child authors' stories) and *Talent Shows* (music, dance and drama inspired by child author's stories).

Chapter 9

Openly stimulating the story!

The box!

Research conducted by OnePoll on behalf of the makers of Ribena Plus (2012) found that children enjoy playing with boxes instead of other toys, gadgets and games. The inspiration for this Idea is credited to Catherine Hetherington who put a box in the middle of a circle of children and got them to think of creative ways of using the box as a way of generating ideas for their story writing. The suggestions below consider the inspirational potential of just two different kinds of cardboard box and merely offer *initial* creative questions to spark imaginations rather than present 'the definitive'!

Lower Key stage 2 – Cereal box

- A hat – *What kind of hat is it? What is the hat made out of? Who is it for? Who finds/loses the hat? Does it fit/suit them? What is special about the hat?*
- A *mi*Pad – *What unique apps are on it? What innovative things can it do? How is it different from an iPad? How do you charge it up? What happens when an unusual message appears on the screen?*
- A box file – *What is stored inside it? Secret papers? Money? Cheat codes for a new computer game? Who does the box file belong to? Where do they keep it? Is it safe there?*
- An artist's canvas – *What does the artist draw/paint on it? How long does it take them to complete the painting/drawing? Where is it displayed? Is it liked or loathed by others? Why?*

See http://tinyurl.com/mcrj4fj for further inspiration.

Upper Key stage 2 – Tissue box

- A monster's shoe – *Where was it found? Who found it? Whose foot/hoof/antennae does it fit? What does the shoe look like? What is it made out of? Why does it 'sparkle'?*
- A bomb – *Who builds it? Why have they built it? Where is it planted? How long before it goes off? Who manages to try to defuse it? What happens when it does explode?*

- A piggy bank – *Who does it belong to? How much money is inside? What else is found inside? What happens when 'the bank' is opened?*
- A giant's smartphone – *Who does she or he call/text? Why does she or he call/text them? What response is given by the receiver of the message/text? Why do they react this way?*

See http://tinyurl.com/kbfu749 for further inspiration and information.

Gold star!

Consider offering child authors a range of other different kinds of boxes (real/images of) to stimulate their story writing e.g. *jewellery, shoe, first-aid, lunch, ring, picnic, bird, fuse, cake, watch, pencil, match, wicker, chocolate, tool, money, juice, music, storage* and *popcorn*. Visit http://tinyurl.com/lek7enj and click on the green Box Picture Gallery link to see the wonderful potential that a simple box can have in the artistic minds of children. *How can this potential be used to fuel child authors' story writing?*

The tube!

Many parents/carers see tubes, particularly those made of cardboard, simply as disposable objects; many professionals (hopefully) see tubes as potential 'gold' for story stimulation! Invite child authors to collect different kinds of tubes from home e.g. *paper towel, cling-film, foil, gift wrap* and *poster* (check whether you are able to use toilet roll tubes in the classroom as there are hygiene issues associated with their potential/actual use). With a little imagination these tubes can really inspire child authors as they talk about them, handle them and write stories about and on them!

Lower Key stage 2

- Telephone – *Who is calling? When do they call? What kind of voice is heard at the other end of the line? What do they say? Is it something exciting/awful? How does the listener react?*
- Antenna – *Is it an insect's (antennae) or one that picks up radio signals (antennas)? What unusual things can the antennae do? How do characters react when they see the size/shape of the antennae?*
- Large drinking straw – *Who does the straw belong to? A monster? A donkey? What are they drinking and what are they drinking out of? How does the drink affect them once they have drunk it?*
- Underwater breathing apparatus – *Who has to/wants to use it? Where is the apparatus used? In the bath? Under the sea? In a lake? How long can the users stay underwater for with the apparatus? What happens to it during their exploration of the body of water?*

Upper Key stage 2

- Remote control – *What does it control? A space rover? The TV? Multiple DVD players? Barriers/gates? What happens when the remote malfunctions? What if the remote loses some buttons or some new ones appear on the control? What can each of them do if pressed?*
- Teleportation tool – *How does it work? Where/when does the person/object using it get transported to? Do they have a choice as to where they 'land'? How/do they change history? By accident or on purpose?*
- GPS tracking device – *In what form is the device? A watch/car/phone/electronic tag? Why is the person/animal/vehicle being tracked? Who is tracking them? What happens when the tracking device breaks or the signal is lost?*

Gold star!

Develop child authors' general knowledge by helping them to recognise other kinds of tubes they may not necessarily be aware of e.g. *display, florescent lighting, hamster, pasta, concrete, vacuum, feeding, inner, tubes for sweets* and *tube slides.* Consider the potential of these tubes in helping to set up problems for characters in child authors' stories when these tubes either break, get a puncture, get blocked, split or shatter! Think about the tubes representing a home for different characters (think *Teenage Mutant Hero/Ninja Turtles*) – *who might be lurking in their abode?*

The hat!

Village Hat Shop (2015) wisely states that 'hats matter' – when we think of the Tin Man (*The Wizard of Oz*) and Sherlock Holmes it is easy to see what makes them such visually distinctive characters. Professionals can help child authors to appreciate how much 'hats matter', not only when thinking about the physical appearance of their characters but also about their potential in relation to stimulating different elements of their written stories such as character and plot.

Lower Key stage 2

- Challenge child authors to write a stimulating story about a character's hat that has been made from the same material as Mary Poppins' famous carpet bag. *What's inside the magic hat that helps the character when they come face to face with a dangerous wild animal in the jungle/a bully on the playground/a tall rope on the obstacle course?* What if Mary Poppins made a 'special appearance' in the story wanting to borrow the hat to help the new family she was nannying for – *how unique would that be?!*
- Suggest that child authors write an antagonistic story about two overly competitive rich friends who fly around the world trying to outdo each other by finding the most outrageous hats they can buy: *'Where do they fly to? What makes the hats they find outrageous? How much do the hats cost? Who manages to eventually*

outdo the other? What do they win?' See *Millie's Marvellous Hat* (Kitamura, 2009) as a source of inspiration.

Upper Key stage 2

- Get child authors to write a 'stolen story' about a first-time thief who steals a hat from a shop but only because their Nan wants a new one for her birthday. When family members start asking lots of questions about the hat, the thief (also a family member) realises they have done wrong and need to 'come clean' about how the hat was really 'purchased'. Explore the different emotions experienced by the thief during the execution of stealing the hat, the giving of it to Nan and the eventual admittance of stealing the hat. *'How do they right the wrong they have done?'*
- Encourage child authors to write a romantic story about a character who decides to send their loved one a hat through the post for Valentine's Day: *'What sort of hat do they choose and why? Does it get to their Valentine safely and on time? Does the recipient like it? Why/why not? What happens when the recipient receives another hat? Is this from a secret admirer? Who are they?'* Consider presenting this story on a paper hat shaped like a heart.

Gold star!

Give child authors the opportunity to become child *designers*, designing (and making, where appropriate) a new hat for a story character. Encourage them to be creative with the style, shape, size, colour(s), fabric(s) and the way in which the hat is worn, ensuring that their decisions reflect or accentuate the personality traits of the character – think *glitter, bright colours, feathers and sequins for a very flamboyant man*. Use this practical designing (and making) experience as useful 'story fodder' for a written tale about a hat-designing competition (local/national) that is won by none other than the child author themselves! *What do they win?*

Fabric!

English and Broadhead (2004: 17) claim that '[c]reativity comes from owning ideas and from seeing possibilities'. Professionals can promote this by simply offering child authors a piece of plain fabric (white, cotton, 3 m × 1 m approx.). Support them in 'seeing possibilities' by playing around with the fabric and manipulating it into different shapes, objects and articles that can be 'owned' by child authors as key items to drive their written stories forwards. Use the ideas below as inspirational suggestion starters!

Lower Key stage 2

- *A ghost* – What sort of ghost is it? A silly/lonely/scary/shy/young one? Where does the ghost 'live'/appear? Why has the ghost appeared?

- *Frothy bubbles* – Who has made them? Where have they been made? In the bath/the sink/a waterfall? Why so? What is special about the bubbles?
- A *desert island* – Who is washed up on the island? Who else inhabits the island? Are they friendly/evil/sly/angry/vengeful/hopeless?
- A *picnic blanket* – What sort of picnic is taking place? Who is attending the picnic? What is there to eat and drink? What happens to ruin the picnic?

Upper Key stage 2

- A *roman toga* – Who is wearing it? Why is it being worn? For a party/as a bet/the wearer has nothing else to wear? What happens when the toga gets torn?
- An *iceberg* – Where is the iceberg – the Antarctic or the Arctic? What/who is living on/in the iceberg? Why? What damage does the iceberg cause? Why is it shrinking?
- A *mummy* – Is it a human or animal one? Where is the mummy found? Who finds it? Does it come to life? What does it say/do?
- A *duvet* – What is the duvet made out of? Who is under/on top of the duvet? Are they sad/asleep/hiding/unwell? What is 'special' about this duvet?

Gold star!

Provide child authors with a range of different types of fabric that they can handle e.g. *silk, felt, mesh, lace, flannel, velvet, linen, wool, satin, gauze, leather, tweed, suede, corduroy, denim* and *faux fur*. Develop and extend vocabularies by getting child authors to describe these fabrics using a blindfold or a feely box, prompting them with new words (see http://tinyurl.com/k9xualw). Encourage child authors to use these adjectives to enrich written descriptions of their characters' clothing and other textured body parts e.g. *soft* skin, *stubbly* chin, *smooth* hands and *furry* legs! For stimulation invite child authors to add these fabrics to their illustrations to create 'sensory sketches'!

The suitcase!

'The suitcase was old and battered and on the side, in large letters, were the words WANTED ON VOYAGE.' Any idea whose famous suitcase Bond (2008: 14) is describing? *That's right – Paddington Bear's!* With suitcases being of story-title importance to the wonderful storytelling of Jacqueline Wilson (*The Suitcase Kid*, 2006), child authors should be given the opportunity to explore the potential that suitcases might have for their own written stories!

Lower Key stage 2

- Get child authors to consider those suitcases that are always left on the baggage carousel at the airport. *Who do they think they belong to?* Invent interesting characters based on stimulating items that might be found in them e.g. *an enormous magnifying glass, a mop with a retractable musical handle, a glittery wireless microphone headset* or *a pair of size 14 trainers.* Write an intriguing story about *why* the suitcase's owner(s) did not collect their suitcase. *'Do they ever get it back? If so, how? Do they* want *it back, though?'*

- Stimulate story climaxes by getting child authors to think about the moment when their lead protagonist opens their suitcase after a *really* long and eventful journey: *'What's inside? Thick foam from a leaking can of hair mousse? A chirping puffin? Fancy dress wigs? Loot from one of* Gangsta Granny's *early heists?'* Consider presenting this surprise as a pop-up visual 'reveal' when preparing the final version of their story for a class anthology – see http://tinyurl.com/oabgadq for ideas.

Upper Key stage 2

- Encourage child authors to use suitcases as an effective 'plot maker' by considering all the different things that could go wrong when a character packs a suitcase in haste e.g. *the handle snaps, a wheel falls off, a zip breaks, the padlock lock will not open* or *the case splits. 'How do protagonists creatively deal with these difficulties when stressed/anxious/in a hurry? Will they make their plane/train on time?'*
- Use *Hana's Suitcase* (Levine, 2003) as a wonderful book to fire children's curiosity and historical knowledge about the Second World War. Stimulating teaching notes written by Prawer – see http://tinyurl.com/nujq7g5 – offer a wealth of story writing possibilities based on the curious empty suitcase: consider offering these to your child authors!

Gold star!

Suitcases can be used to excite child authors' story writing not only at school but also at home – see http://tinyurl.com/kvmp9w5 for a wonderful American-based family literacy project for young children that uses a *writing suitcase*. Adapt this by using *writing rucksacks* (7–9) and *weekend writing bags* (9–11) which serve as age-appropriate alternatives for those in LKS2 and UKS2 respectively. This is a particularly useful idea for professionals who work with child authors in deprived areas. Alternatively, promote the idea of *No Pen Wednesday* every day at home! See http://tinyurl.com/lc96xdp for information.

Timepiece!

'Hickory dickory dock, the mouse ran up the clock…' Have you ever wondered what sort of clock it was? Illustrations that accompany this well-known nursery rhyme suggest that it was a grandfather clock. With a bit of imagination though it *could* be Big Ben, the famous clock in London or it *could* be a carriage clock with a baby/dwarf mouse! Child authors can use timepieces (examples of which are offered overleaf) as a useful resource for stimulating their stories as the following ideas so aptly suggest!

Mobile/smart phone	Desktop clock	Bedroom alarm clock	Pocket watch
Nurse's fob watch	Musical clock	Digital stop watch	Cuckoo clock
Kitchen wall clock	Wrist watch	Microwave clock	Water clock
Speaking clock	Hourglass	Oil lamp clock	Egg timer

Lower Key stage 2

- Show child authors an age-appropriate newspaper. *'Imagine that the lead protagonist in your impending story is reading it one morning when they come across a small article which states that the world is going to end at 15.27 that day. How does your lead protagonist react to this? What do they do from the moment of reading the article until 15.27? What happens at precisely 15.27?'* Use *Doctor Who* as inspiration for some exciting 'up-to-the-minute' story writing!
- Challenge child authors to draft small paragraphs/sections of their time-related stories against an actual time limit. Visit http://tinyurl.com/6tq73bu for some online child-friendly timepieces (timers) which can be displayed on the IWB as your child authors work, taking care that this does not put them under any unnecessary pressure.

Upper Key stage 2

- Offer child authors the story title *The House of Upset Time.* Talk to them about there being an old house at the top of the hill that has a different timepiece in each room which tells a different time. The decor of each room represents a different time period e.g. the Second World War, the Swinging Sixties, the Victorian era. *'Who stumbles across this old house? Who does this house belong to? What happens to story characters when they enter each room? How do they escape the house and do they manage to re-enter their own time?'*
- Help child authors to understand the notion of the Butterfly Effect by showing them the Simpson's Halloween episode *Time and Punishment* (see *YouTube*). Get child authors to consider how a minor change in circumstances in their story e.g. *someone's timepiece gets accidentally broken* subsequently causes a large change in the outcome of the tale e.g. *everything in the world turns into blue blancmange!*

Gold star!

Research carried out by YouGov for education publishers Pearson (cited in Paton, 2012) revealed that one-in-six mothers and fathers admit that they never read to their children before bedtime. Encourage child authors to read/talk about *their* written stories (be they initial ideas, 'work in progress' or the final draft) to their parents/carers before they go to sleep at night whenever possible in an effort to positively address this concerning statistic. Alternatively, get parents/carers and child authors to orally create stories together as part of their bedtime routine to promote and hone storymaking and storytelling skills (see Cutspec, 2006).

The bottle!

'[Alice] went back to the table...this time she found a little bottle on it...round the neck of the bottle was a paper label, with the words "DRINK ME" beautifully printed on it in large letters.' Carroll (2008: 16) famously used the contents of the little bottle to help change the physical size of his well-known protagonist. Think about the story potential that the contents of different bottles could have in the creative minds of child authors – *characters could grow wings, change colour, turn into stone, develop superpowers, speak 17 languages* or *become invisible*. Other exciting 'bottled' ideas that professionals can use to stimulate child authors' story writing include...

Lower Key stage 2

- Invite child authors to create a *Story in a Bottle* (adapted from Brownhill, 2013: 63). Imagine that they are on a desert island and the only thing they have to help them pass the time is a pencil, a piece of paper and a plastic bottle: '*What kind of story will you write?*' If possible, 'release' the stories into the nearby stream/lake/ river/sea. *Who might find the bottle? Where might it be found? What might they think of the story?* Consider including the school address to see if they get a reply!
- Read the beautiful story *The Heart and the Bottle* (Jeffers, 2011). Encourage child authors to write a sensitive story about a character that puts a different part of their body in a bottle to protect it from being hurt again e.g. *brain, hand, ear* or *foot*. '*How does this affect the subsequent days/weeks/years/life of the character? Was it a mistake to protect it in this way?*'

Upper Key stage 2

- Talk with child authors about the dangers of 'bottling up' one's emotions. Challenge them to write an emotional story about a character that does this and the effects that this has on their behaviour towards others. Explore through PHSCE opportunities healthy ways to release emotions (see Sunderland, 2001 for strategies and ideas). '*Could these be suggested by other characters in their story to help the protagonist? Which of these suggestions actually work and how do they help the lead character?*'
- Get child authors to research different materials which have been/are used to make bottles e.g. *plastic, glass, aluminium* and *clay*. In their extended stories suggest that they use these materials to influence the story plot e.g. *bottles get broken* (glass), *the contents seep into the bottle* (clay), *the bottle affects its contents in some way* (plastic, aluminium). '*What new materials do characters try to make bottles out of to prevent the above from occurring? Paper/cardboard/stone/ fabric/wood? How effective are they?*'

Gold star!

In the summers of 2013 and 2014 Coca-Cola replaced its iconic logo on its bottles with over 1,000 of the most popular names in Great Britain as part of its *Share a Coke with…* campaign. Invite child authors to take part in a class/school *Share a story with…* campaign which involves them writing a story, popping it into a recyclable plastic bottle and attaching a waterproof sticky label to its side on which is written '*Share a story with* _____' (enter the name of a different child author here). Put the bottled stories into a sink/water tray (LKS2) or a paddling pool (UKS2), select a bottle using a net, and find the child author who the bottle 'belongs to', sharing the written story with them.

String!

Children are known for asking some wonderful questions. Professionals are also known for giving wonderful answers in response to these! Take a look at this classic exchange between a child and their teacher:

Child: How long should my story be, Miss?
Teacher: It should be as long as a piece of string!

Professionals can use string as a versatile resource to stimulate and support child authors' story writing in their classrooms, practical ideas of which are offered below!

Lower Key stage 2

* Develop story writing collaborations by cutting up string so that there are a small number of pieces (between two and four) that are the same length. Upon taking a piece each ask child authors to find and write with those people who have the same length of string as theirs. Get them to think about the role of string in their story: '*What might story characters make out of it e.g. a miniature ladder/skipping rope/net/necklace/belt/strap/washing line? Why is this needed?*'
* Offer child authors a piece of string along with small pieces of coloured paper, pens and a hole-punch. Use these to create a physical timeline to help them plot a 'dark' (horror) story, threading the paper with written ideas on onto the string using an agreed colour key e.g. yellow = *the sensational opener*, green = *the main 'troubled' protagonist*, red = *an unusual setting* etc. Ensure that child authors make regular reference to it during the writing of their initial draft.

Upper Key stage 2

* Distribute pieces of string that have a different number of knots (small/large) along them. Get child authors to imagine these knots represent individual story problems (minor = small; major = big). Challenge them to write a 'knotty' [complex]

story which is fuelled by the number of knots in their string, distributing these problems across different story chapters.

- Get child authors to shape a piece of string into a single loop (a circle) or a series of loops. Explain that the circle/each circle represents a 'time loop', a common plot device in time travel stories where a period of time – *a few hours or a few days* – repeats again and again (think *Doctor Who* and the film *Groundhog Day*). Get child authors to write a story that involves one of their characters realising they are in a loop and escaping it by recognising some key truth or correcting one of their past mistakes e.g. *being unpleasantly rude to someone who subsequently died* or *having to study hard to pass a science test*.

Gold star!

Storytellers such as Ruth Stotter and David Titus strongly advocate the use of string when telling stories. See pp. 3–45 of Pellowski's *The Story Vine* (available at http://tinyurl.com/mgqe6xs) which serves as 'a source book of unusual and easy-to-tell stories from around the world' (p. i) that use string. Model how to tell these stories in the classroom by using and adapting Pellowski's guidance, challenging child authors to verbalise their own written stories to parents/carers at home with string as part of an oral homework activity.

The present!

Offer any child a wrapped present and professionals are likely to immediately engage their interest: *'I wonder what's inside?'* This curiosity can be captured in child authors' stories if they are encouraged to write about gifts and the many activities associated with them e.g. *deciding what to get and how much to spend, the wrapping, the giving and receiving, the recipient's reaction* and *the subsequent use of the gift*. It is argued that there is nothing better than giving/receiving a story book as a present – *perhaps child authors might write one instead of having to always raid their piggy bank or ask their parents/carers to buy a gift!*

Lower Key stage 2

- Show child authors a congratulations card: *'What occasions might this be given to people for?'* Suggest that child authors write a story about a story character who buys a totally inappropriate gift for the occasion: *'How does the recipient react when they open it? What do they do with it "after the event"? Return it to the shop? Sell it on eBay? Give it away? What happens when the main character finds out? How do they feel?'*
- Talk to child authors about the notion of random acts of kindness – see http://tinyurl.com/opomyca. Invite child authors to write a sweet story about a character who decides to give a gift a day as a random act of kindness to seven different characters: *'Who are these characters? Why are they given a gift? What do they receive? Do they like what they have been given? How does this make each of the*

recipients feel? What does the main character get in return?' Might child authors subsequently decide to take part in National Kindness Day?

Upper Key stage 2

- Suggest that child authors write a faith-orientated story about gift-giving as part of a religious celebration/holiday e.g. *Christians and Christmas, Muslims and the end of Ramadan, Jews and Hanukkah, Hindus and Diwali* or *Buddhists and Vesak.* Use this story as an opportunity to 'educate the reader' with cultural information interspersed throughout the funny tale about amusing things that happen when certain gifts are opened e.g. *people being frightened/shocked/ surprised and jumping/laughing/crying as a result. 'What could be in the wrapping/gift box to make them react this way?'*
- Draw a straight line on the IWB, asking child authors to indicate where they think certain events appear on the 'life line' of a character e.g. birth (at the start), wedding (near the middle), death (at the end). Get child authors to write an intriguing sci-fi story in which time travels backwards, meaning that the main character regresses from being an old man/woman to becoming a baby. *What gifts do they get at different points of their receding life and how do these items become useless or inappropriate as they decrease in age?*

Gold star!

It is suggested that dreams are a rich source of inspiration for writers – think Shakespeare's *A Midsummer Night's Dream* (Matthews, 2003). Encourage child authors to 'capture' dreams through conversations with peers and professionals, drawings/sketches, key 'trigger' words and written sentences presented in clouds, stars or dreamcatcher templates. Use these as the basis for a fantasy story about dreams that come true, dreams that are stolen or adventures that characters have that were 'just a dream'.

Story writing 'pick and mix' 9

Here is a ninth and penultimate collection of stimulating story writing ideas to engage child authors and enrich professional practices. As explained in 'Story writing "pick and mix" 1' (see pp. 20–21) this assortment of ideas is not attributed to a particular age phase but is offered more as a selection of suggestions for professionals to choose from and adapt in response to the writing needs of their learners – *put an 'X' by any that you think you might try out!*

X

↓

Story switch: Show child authors how to create a new story by 'switching' individual words in the titles of published stories e.g. *Give Peas A Chance* (Gleitzman, 2008) becomes *Give Ventriloquists a Chance*; *The Parent Agency* (Baddiel, 2014) become *The Sibling Agency*. Now they have the title, all they need to do is write the story!
Facts into story fiction: Offer child authors a range of age-appropriate facts from the BBC *QI* series, inviting them to use these as stimulation for their story writing e.g. 'Polo mints release light when you snap them' (Lloyd *et al.*, 2014: 80): *'What could be released when Tommy breaks open the gobstopper Grampy bought him? A dragon? Talking jelly? Liquid gold? A book?'*
Story world records: Invite child authors to invent some outrageous new *Guinness World Records* that their story characters want to set e.g. *creating the biggest bogey mountain* or *sitting in a bath of hundreds and thousands for a week.* Support them in considering different dilemmas which threaten the successful completion of the world record e.g. *not finding enough people with a cold* or *needing to go to the toilet!*
Story shapes: Help child authors to create different 3D shapes out of paper using nets (see http://tinyurl.com/otwtq62). Support them in using selected shapes as stimuli for their story e.g. a *pyramid* (a story set in Ancient Egypt) or a *cone* (a story about a witch, the cone representing their hat). **Remember:** encourage them to present their written story on the *outside* of the net prior to building it!
Prezi story: Give child authors the opportunity to move away from the comfort of using *PowerPoint* to experimenting with *Prezi* as an exciting way to present their written story to others. Visit http://tinyurl.com/nzoglez for ideas on how to help child authors build tension and suspense in their stories, using *Prezi* as a teaching tool.
Story peculiarities: Present child authors with two intriguing titles: *The Day After Yesterday* and *The Day Before Tomorrow.* Clever child authors will deduce that the titles refer to *today!* Get them to write stories in the present tense using selected forms depending on their abilities e.g. simple, progressive, perfect and perfect progressive (see Uchiyama, 2006).

Chapter 10

Getting started!

Tremendous titles!

Child authors can write the most wonderful story that can be 'wrapped up' in a beautifully self-designed front cover, but if the story title does not grab the reader's attention then they [the reader] are unlikely to want to read it! Story titles such as *The Life Cycle of the Flea* and *Sammy's 29th Boring Day at the Bus Stop* just do not cut it; story titles should embrace the 3Cs rule: *catchy*, *concise* and *curious*. Share with child authors the suggested titles below to both exemplify the 3Cs rule and stimulate their story writing.

Lower Key stage 2		
Tutu Tuesday!	The time-travelling tea-towel!	The Helicopter and the Hurricane
Sleepover under the stars!	When the circus left town	'Did you shut the front door?'
A Song for Suzie	Peter in Pieces!	Seventh time lucky!
Dark Door	My illustrative imp!	Candy Land

Upper Key stage 2		
The Story Jumper	Results Day!	The Boy with Two Backs
The Mystery of the Ice-Cream Footprints	Eating my shirt buttons!	The Night of the Exploding Biscuit Tins!
The Prince and the Pelican	Temper, Temper!	Danny's Duvet Day
Cold hands	The Smell of Terror	Getting the balance right

Show child authors how to 'unpick the possibilities' of suggested story titles by modelling the process of thought showering *questions for consideration* <u>around</u> the title on an easel/IWB. Some examples are given overleaf.

How messy is Messy Max – just a little or really messy?	What does Max physically look like? How old is he?	Could Max actually be a girl – Max<u>ine</u>?
Does Max want to be part of the Spring Clean? Why / not? How does he try to avoid it? Does he succeed?	**Messy Max and the Spring Clean**	What does Max have to spring clean? His bedroom? How do we [the reader] know that it needs to be spring cleaned?
Is there anyone else involved in the Spring Clean e.g. Mum? Dad? Brothers and sisters?	What specific month / day does the Spring Clean take place on? Is it important to know this?	Who asks / makes Max take part in the Spring Clean? What does Max find during the clean?

Invite child authors to select story books from the book corner/box/library (school/local)/their home collection or from online lists, sorting these into titles that they like and dislike. Get them to explain *why* they like particular titles, noting down and displaying these reasons – these can be used as a useful aide memoire of what makes a 'good' story title e.g. 'snappy' one-word named titles (*Matilda*), alliterative titles (*Peter Pan*), or those that use onomatopoeic words (*Boom!*).

Note!

Maynard (2002: 99) found that children's difficulties in coming up with 'good ideas' for their story writing can actually stem from 'the…teachers' choice of story title'. Professionals should be encouraged to offer a *balance of provision*, letting child authors write with a 'free mind' so that they can use *their* 'good ideas' to maintain their 'enthusiasm' for story writing.

Gold star!

Show child authors how to 'tweak' well-known children's story titles to create new ones which they can use as stimuli for their own tales e.g.:

Key stage	Well-known story title	'Tweaked' story title
LKS2	The Lion, the Witch and the Wardrobe	The Star, the Fish and the Flagpole
	Pongwiffy	Smelly Nelly
UKS2	The Graveyard Book	The Department Store Ledger
	Scribbleboy	Doodlegirl

If child authors struggle to initially decide on a 'cracking' story title suggest that they offer a temporary *working title* that can be changed once their story is complete (think *Blue Harvest* for the film *Star Wars: Return of the Jedi*). Alternatively, they could give their story a secretive title such as *Project H* until it 'goes public' (is read by others).

A sentence starter for 10!

Moore (2005: 2) suggests that 'a lack of varied sentence starters [in children's writing is] a source of endless frustration in the writing process' – without this variety child authors' stories can become repetitive and dull: *And then...and...and...and...!* Professionals can stimulate child authors' storytelling/writing by offering them/ modelling a wealth of *sentence starters/stems/openings* to 'pick and choose' from, using the display strategies also advocated below:

Lower Key stage 2		Display strategies
• Because...	• Even though...	• On clouds/paper raindrops hung from a mobile
• If...	• Meanwhile...	
• When...	• Before very long...	• On individual cue cards
• As...	• However...	• Under window/door/cat flaps on 2D house sheets
• While...	• Grinning...	
• Smiling...	• Shaking...	• On wooden blocks (cubes, cuboids)
• Laughing...	• Exhausted...	• On map or star outlines
• Running...	• Terrified...	• On spiral-shaped/cut paper
• Weeping...	• Annoyed...	• On bricks that make up a wall

Note that many of the sentence opener suggestions offered above and below can be found in the document *Literacy Curricular Targets: Sentence Openers* which is available at: http://tinyurl.com/o9hfx6n. These relate to the VCOP features associated with Ros Wilson's *Big Writing* (see http://tinyurl.com/ocrentr for more information).

Upper Key stage 2		Display strategies
• Tired of waiting...	• Despite James' plan to..., in reality he...	• On individual rainbow beams
• Despite...		• On hot-air balloons/cocktail umbrella covers
• If/then...	• Due to the lack of...my first thought was to...	
• In addition...		• On envelopes stored in handmade red post boxes
• Due to...	• As the weather had become quite stormy we decided to...	
• As time went...		• On bookmarks (fabric)
• Although I had thought that..., I discovered...	• Before the audience left the actors asked...	• On hand lenses (think Sherlock Holmes)
• Having decided to..., I actually...		• On paper kites and bows

Other sentence starters can be found in *Progression in Language Structures* (Tower Hamlets EMA Team in collaboration with Tower Hamlets teachers, 2009). Further examples of sentence starters to encourage older child authors to use include:

• Secondly...	• Silently...
• Once...	• Carefully...
• On...	• Regardless of...
• They...	• Fortunately...
• During...	• Unfortunately...
• So...	• The last time...
• As soon as...	• Late that night...
• From now on...	• Another time...

Consider displaying these on *paper plates, leaflets, the labels on empty bottles, stones (chalked on), old CDs, badges (self-made), luggage tags, face towels (stitched on)* or *mugs (painted on)*.

Gold star!

Engage child authors in sentence-making games to stimulate and enrich their story writing. Useful resources can be found at the following websites:

• http://tinyurl.com/ n2vc442	• http://tinyurl.com/ y9fbb9p	• http://tinyurl.com/ axa4gkv

Alternatively, for those child authors who just need an opening sentence to 'get them off the writing blocks', visit http://tinyurl.com/yke6mh8 for 194,480+ choices that can be adapted and used for their storytelling and story writing!

Curiouser and curiouser!

Carroll's (2008) famous Alice uttered the words which make up the title of this Idea. They seemingly serve as the inspiration for Babauta (2008) who suggests that to create a great beginning to a story authors need to 'Get them [readers] curious. Beyond just getting their attention, you have to arouse their curiosity, so that you can hold their attention, and get them to want to read more. Be different.' Professionals should therefore encourage child authors to write story openers that are purposefully intriguing and yet a little odd!

Lower Key stage 2

•   Pattison (2010) claims that '[s]ometimes a novel begins with a line that is misleading'. Support child authors in writing peculiar opening lines which will make the reader stop and reread it ('Did I read that right?') e.g. *The sun and the moon rose in the sky at the same time*; *Rain fell horizontally towards the drenched castle that was covered in cushions; The crackling fire cooled the old fireman's feet.*

- Freeman (2011) suggests that authors should 'introduce an intriguing character' to grab the attention of the reader. Help child authors to 'zone in' on one particular aspect of their physical appearance/personality that is rather strange and describe this as the curious opener to a historical story e.g. *Ethel deliberately wiped her runny nose along the back of her dirty hands as she kneaded the bread dough in preparation for the Master's lunch; Before Elizabeth was taken to be hanged she kissed her lucky fingernail and secretly rubbed butter all around her neck.*

Upper Key stage 2

- Get child authors to generate some unusual questions which could serve as a curious opener for their written adventure story e.g. *Why did Mr. Peril smile when he saw his turbo car on its roof in the car park? What made Katie decide that she wanted to be a cactus when she grew up? How did Ms. Maguire become the most HATED teacher in the history of the world?*
- Visit http://tinyurl.com/mr4v9lk which offers the '100 best opening lines from children's books'. Get child authors to select one, modelling how it can be altered/amended to make a bizarre opener for their written story e.g. 'Johnny never knew for certain why he started seeing the dead' (*Johnny and the Dead*; Pratchett, 2013: 3) could become 'Jackson knew for certain why his doting sister had started painting her teeth purple'.

Gold star!

There are times when child authors should be encouraged to 'cheat' a little when writing their stories – think Corbett's *Nick the Magpie* (see http://tinyurl.com/pz69uty)! This *does not* mean that they should deliberately plagiarise another author's work but instead should make use of professional-selected 'quick-fire' writing tips/guidance/strategies/advice offered on the *Cheat Sheets* available at http://tinyurl.com/2edpfrs and http://tinyurl.com/kfjbttf. Select and adapt these suggestions for the benefit of the child authors you work with, offering these in verbal and written form via teaching points, displays and summative comments.

Posing a question!

Stephen King (in Fassler, 2013) is adamant that '[a]n opening line should invite the reader to begin the story. It should say: Listen. Come in here. You want to know about this.' One way that this can be achieved is by posing a question to the reader. Child authors can use this not only as an interesting opening 'hook' to initiate their stimulating story, but also as a way of assessing their 'attention grabbing' writing skills by observing readers reading their story (if possible) – if they *keep on* reading then their question was a success!

Lower Key stage 2

- Get child authors to find examples of children's stories which open with a question e.g. 'Ever had the feeling your life's been flushed down the toilet?' (*The Toilet of Doom*, Lawrence, 2001: 5); 'Where's Papa going with that axe?' (*Charlotte's Web*, White, 2003: 1). Display these using ICT applications, encouraging child authors to adapt these as opening questions for their own stories e.g. *Ever had the feeling your belly button has a life of its own? 'What's Mr. Banks doing with that match, Granny?'*
- Support child authors in developing an understanding of rhetorical questions (ones that do not need an answer – see http://tinyurl.com/ofq86pc for some interesting examples!). Offer child authors various unfinished rhetorical question stems for them to creatively complete and use as the opener for a story that takes place underground e.g.

Have you ever...?	Am I the only one who...?	Haven't you always longed for a...?
Fancy...?	When were you last bored by...?	Why does Mum always insist on...?

Upper Key stage 2

- Share with the class this fantastic question opening: 'Have you ever wondered why things happen the way they do? Is there *something* or *someone* manipulating us like we're little toy figures? Well, let me tell how I know what really happens and why.' (See http://tinyurl.com/pmodvmb.) Encourage child authors to thought shower the endless story possibilities that this opening offers, writing their own individual story based on the same opening question given for the whole class. *How creative can they be?*
- Peat (2010b) proposes the 'direct address' method of combining a direct address and a question in the opening sentence to create an empathic response from the reader: *Have you ever wondered what it might be like to fall from a plane and not have your parachute open? Let me describe it for you!* Encourage child authors to use this method to influence the opening of their story e.g. *I bet you've never had a box of cereal attack you in the supermarket, have you? Well, I have, and if you keep on reading I'll tell you why it attacked me!* (Sanjeet, 11.2 yrs).

Gold star!

Role play areas have long been an effective and engaging feature of learning spaces for young children (EYFS). Cremin *et al.* (2008) strongly advocate the use of role play areas in KS1 and KS2 classrooms to support quality learning and teaching. Work with child authors to create and enrich purposeful spaces for story writing e.g. *The Writers' Room, Parable Publishers, The Authors' Atrium* or *The Story Shed* in which child authors can work-in-role *as* 'real' authors. See http://tinyurl.com/p8a6msh for information and some exciting ideas.

Sensory stimulation!

Many child authors will be familiar with *Mr. Potato Head*, the American toy that appeared as an animated character in the *Toy Story* films. A number of plastic parts which can be attached to his body represent the organs that allow us to see, smell, touch, taste and hear (*eyes, nose, hands (skin), mouth (tongue)* and *ears*). These senses, along with others, play an essential role in our lives and can be used to stimulate and enrich child authors' story writing (see http://tinyurl.com/l7ptx3p).

Lower Key stage 2

- Use the power of *smell* to help child authors hint at a problem that their characters are to encounter in their danger-orientated story e.g. *a fire (smoke), a leak (gas)* or *tainted food (smelly sausages!)*. Explain how smells can be used to evoke memories e.g. *when Jenny smells the vanilla scent on her teacher's clothing it reminds her of listening to old gramophone records at Grandma's house*. Smells can also be used to enhance descriptions of settings e.g. *the damp, dank woods that Toby the sweaty dog runs into*, along with the aroma given off by characters: '*Do they have body odour? Are they doused in perfume/aftershave? How does this affect the way that protagonists react to them?*'
- It is believed that *pain* is another sense in addition to Aristotle's 'five'. Receptors of this include the skin, bones and joints and body organs. Show child authors how to elicit sympathy from readers by describing the physical pain that characters have to endure as a result of accidents (*sunburnt skin*), old age (*creaking joints*) or illness (*appendicitis*) in their story about a battle, tests of endurance or after an epic journey/conquest (think *The Hobbit*): '*Is the pain experienced aching/biting/ constant/dull/intense/niggling/penetrating/scratchy/stinging/tiring?*'

Upper Key stage 2

- Emphasise the sense of *temperature* in child authors' stories (various types) by recommending that child authors indicate how protagonists feel, temperature wise, in response to their setting (*the ice cold Arctic*), sounds they hear (*the blood curdling scream that chilled Carrie to the bone*), situations they find themselves in (*flustered by an unwanted kiss*) or illness (*'burning up'*).
- The sense of *balance* can be useful to child authors who wish to develop descriptive passages in their stories about the way characters sense different body movements, direction and acceleration in relation to different events they experience e.g. *running away from a bully, chasing after a thief* or *riding on the back of a frightened horse*. Consider how characters try to attain and maintain postural equilibrium and balance as babies, old people or those recovering from injury: '*How does this affect their movements and self-esteem?*'

Gold star!

Engage child authors in practical activities that stimulate their senses using blindfolds, feely boxes, sound CDs, food samples and smelling pots (see http://tinyurl.com/lwxzzno for other ideas), drawing on these experiences to stimulate and enhance their story writing. Explore the website http://tinyurl.com/nasojqc, inviting child authors to collaborate together to create a *multisensory* story which could be shared with children and adults in the local community who have learning difficulties.

Onomatopoeic 'explosion'!

It is said that if you want to grab the attention of your reader you should start your story off with a bang – that is exactly what Bethany Curtis-Christie did with her competition winning story entitled *Bang!* (Hawkinge Primary School, 2013). Whether they are used as a title (*Boom!*), the name of a story character (*Mr. Bump*) or as a sound effect (*SPLASH!*), onomatopoeic 'explosions' – words that imitate the sound they describe when pronounced – can be an effective way of both gaining and retaining child authors' readers! Exciting examples include:

Boom!	Thud!	Sssshblamm!	Dink!
Twang!	Dhummm!	Whizz!	Neee Narrr!
Pffffhhhhh!	Kapow!	Thump!	Ping!
Wallop!	Slurp!	Kkkkhhhhh!	Crash!
Clatter!	Rarrrrr!	Ding Dong!	Splat!

Encourage child authors to consider using these 'explosion' words in their stories by using the following ideas and suggestions.

Lower Key stage 2

*   Show child authors how onomatopoeic explosions can be used in their spooky stories to scare readers using capital letters e.g. *Suddenly there was an almighty* CRASH *and then the awful low sound of* moaning *and* groaning *coming from the dark landing.* Encourage child authors to use other techniques of presenting their onomatopoeic explosions on the page e.g. *in different coloured pens, in **bold**/italic font* or <u>underlined</u>.
*   Suggest that child authors offer an onomatopoeic explosion as the opening to their sporty story – *Whack!*; **DONG!**; <u>PING!</u> Model how they can explain what or who made the sound and why the sound was made in the first sentence or introductory paragraph to satisfy the reader's curiosity e.g. '*Would you believe it?!* Marty hit yet *another* tennis ball over the next door neighbour's fence!'

Upper Key stage 2

- Show child authors *Batman Fight Scenes using Onomatopoeia* on *YouTube* from the 1960s TV show *Batman* (see http://tinyurl.com/moqsy5u). Encourage them to offer onomatopoeic explosions during written descriptions of any fights or battles that involve their protagonist(s), be they friendly or deliberately brutal (think myths and legends in terms of conflict with dragons and monsters).
- Using ICT software, allow child authors to experiment with the presentation of onomatopoeic words that appear in their horror story, varying the appearance of these to accentuate their explosiveness and value in the scary storytelling as the 'horror-filled antagonist' first appears e.g.

RARRRRRRR! or KABOOOOOOOOM!

Gold star!

Help child authors to develop a bank of useful onomatopoeic words by adapting the lyrics to the song *Old MacDonald* for younger children e.g. *And on that farm he had some <u>bells</u> ... with a <u>DING DONG</u> here...; And on that farm he had some <u>drinks</u>...with a <u>SLURP SLURP</u> here...* Alternatively, develop child authors' understanding and appreciation of onomatopoeia using comic books/strips or onomatopoeic pop art as a visual teaching resource.

Let me introduce myself!

Kendell (2004: 23) suggests that child authors can open a story by 'talk[ing] directly to the reader'. While Freeman (2010) finds this 'annoying', dialogue which is directed to the reader can be effective in both breaking down the 'fourth wall' (see http://tinyurl.com/l74ay4n for information) and attracting their attention so that they want to 'read on'. Support child authors in thinking about different ways of 'speaking' to readers that will intrigue and draw them into the tale that they [child authors] want to tell/write.

Lower Key stage 2

- Get child authors to create a 'complimentary character', one who constantly flatters everyone with praise and approval. Invite them to try and 'butter up' the reader with an admiring comment at the start of their story e.g. *I do like your hair!*; *I wish I had teeth like you!*; *Those clothes you are wearing really suit you!* Explore as part of the story whether these remarks are genuine or whether there is an ulterior motive behind their words of approval. *Do they say things like this to worm their way into people's lives/wallets/houses?*
- Get child authors to generate questions and statements which start with the word 'You' e.g. *<u>You</u> might be wondering why...*; *<u>You</u> haven't got any spare change for a cup of tea, have you?*; *<u>You</u> do make me laugh, you know!* Invite them to use one of these to open a crime-based story in which the narrator is clearly the main character of the tale (and possibly the thief/pick pocket/assassin!).

Upper Key stage 2

- Invite child authors to generate a list of exclamations which are deliberately provocative e.g. *I hate you!*; *You make me want to be sick!*; *I cannot stand the sight of you!*; *You're toxic!* Suggest that child authors present one of these as the opening to a written story which is directed at the reader. *'Is the exclamation a true reflection of the character's nature or are they just having a bad day?'* Explore this as part of the telling of the turbulent tale.

- Talk to child authors about how opening lines can mystify the reader e.g. *He swallowed the dice and then shook himself to try and get a double six*; *The dog licked the door and hummed*; *David put the drain pipe under his arm and ran at the wall.* Get child authors to create a sincere 'address' to the reader which purposefully puzzles them e.g. *I know you live in a suitcase like me*; *The hairs on the back of your hand are really radio antennas, you know!*; *'How does the rest of the story aim to unravel the puzzle?'*

Gold star!

Effective professionals, like child authors, are like magpies that take good ideas and utilise them as part of their own practice. Enrich your direct-taught input by using and adapting the suggested online story writing resources below:

LKS2	Roald Dahl story openings	http://tinyurl.com/m5llt9r
	Narrative And Stories	http://tinyurl.com/ltavlxu
UKS2	'Developing Creative Writing Skills'	http://tinyurl.com/o8mm3sj
	Checklist for effective narrative writing	http://tinyurl.com/mtxenz4

Lights! Camera! Action!

Professionals will recognise the title of this Idea as the traditional cue for a movie crew at the beginning of a 'take'. Pullman (2012: xiv) asserts that '[a] good tale moves like a dreamlike speed from event to event, pausing only to say as much as is needed'. With this in mind child authors should be encouraged to write stories which incorporate lots of 'swiftness', not just to benefit the story plot but also those who can be encouraged to be *physically active* when reading it.

Lower Key stage 2

- Initially engage child authors in speedy 'Total Physical Response games such as *Simon Says* and songs like *Head, Shoulders, Knees and Toes*' (Jones, 2012: 1). Build on this by teaching them simple stories that they can hear and act out – see http://tinyurl.com/pf4chhc (pp. 2–3). Encourage child authors to then carefully write their own action story for a younger audience, actively sharing this with children in the EYFS as part of an 'Active Writing Showcase'.

- Offer individual child authors one of the 50 visual story boards by Gerngross and Puchta (1996 – see http://tinyurl.com/ltvvfw7, p. 26+). Get them to think about the dialogue which might take place during the depicted story: *'How could you use action verbs to describe the speech that commences your "story with a tempo" e.g. rather than having your character "shout" get them to bawl, bay, bellow, cheer, clamour, exclaim, holler, roar, scream, screech, shriek, squall, squawk, whoop, yammer, yap or yell!'* Encourage them to integrate these verbs appropriately in their dialogue-heavy story of two characters arguing about where to go on holiday together. *'Do they eventually manage to decide where to go?'*

Upper Key stage 2

- An effective way to 'fire up' an action story is to get straight into the action which Peat (2010b) refers to as *In medias res*. Support child authors in generating lively 'starter sentences' which throw the reader straight into the story e.g. *Her dirty left shoe struck my leg as I stumbled and fell to the wet floor* or *In the dead of night the boat set sail in search of the underbelly of the world.* See http://tinyurl.com/k5d6eln for further ideas.
- Visit http://tinyurl.com/d6f9ay9, paying particular attention to pp. 43–44. Use these exemplar materials to stimulate discussion as to how child authors can structure sentences, use punctuation and organise the text to make the '[a]ction burst on to the page' (DfES, 2002: 44). Get them to utilise these strategies in an action-based story that focuses on a curse, the effects of a new medicine / drug, a dangerous game of hide and seek or a violent volcanic eruption.

Gold star!

While busy professionals are understandably more interested in the WHAT and HOW of story writing it is important to sometimes consider the WHY of story writing (child authors also need to know this as they progress in their abilities!). Read *Vygotsky and the Teaching of Writing* (Everson, 1991), reflecting critically on the content of the article as part of your IPD / CPD. *How is the narrative practice in your classroom underpinned by theoretical understanding?* Alternatively, see http://tinyurl.com/msovlsk for a wealth of writing stories resources to support the HOW of story writing in KS2 classrooms.

Get the picture!

Cleese (2014: 140) asserts that any young writer should 'steal an idea that you know is good, and try to reproduce it in a setting that you know and understand'. While the idea of actively encouraging child authors to directly plagiarise others' work is *strongly* discouraged in this book (see p. 129), a dedicated attempt has been made overleaf to creatively *adapt* a wealth of interesting ideas to stimulate children's story writing. The title of this Idea mirrors that of the 1990s' Nickelodeon children's game show *Get The*

Picture; the activities described are 'tweaked' from the games that were played during this engaging American programme.

Lower Key stage 2

- *Extreme Close-Up:* Give child authors an image from a magazine/catalogue/book with a piece of card that covers the entire image apart from a small square/circle/rectangle/triangle that is cut out somewhere in the card (think of a view finder). Get child authors to decipher what they think the full image is, using this as the stimulus for a sad story. Remove the 'covering card' at the end to see if the image is suitable as the front cover for their story!
- *Word Up:* Offer child authors a word search puzzle (self-created/internet-based). Invite them to find as many hidden words as they can. Get them to guess what *theme* the words relate to – *love/magic/loss/adventure?* Challenge them to write an intriguing story which is based on the correctly identified theme, weaving each of the found words into their extended tale.

Upper Key stage 2

- *Airport Security:* Get child authors to write a story about a work experience opportunity at the local airport. Encourage them to describe different passengers and their luggage that pass through airport security: *'What can you see when their belongings go through the X-ray machine? What happens when one of the passengers tries to take something on the plane which they are not allowed?'* See http://tinyurl.com/k5lu4vn for initial ideas!
- *Visual Distortion:* Get child authors to write a story about some friends who go to the travelling fairground and have fun looking at themselves in the crazy mirrors which twist and distort their image. Once they get outside – *shock, horror!* – they find that their bodies for some reason actually mirror the images that they saw! *'How do the friends manage to get themselves back to normal?'*

Gold star!

Famous authors such as Michael Morpurgo, Margaret Atwood, Philip Pullman, Roddy Doyle and P.D. James were asked to list their ten rules for writing fiction as inspired by Leonard's (2010) *10 Rules of Writing*. Visit http://tinyurl.com/kvjlxjq and http://tinyurl.com/nrlwm7o, identifying which of the 230+ rules presented you would adapt/share/advocate with your child authors to practically support their story writing development. Encourage older child authors to formulate their own rules of writing, comparing these to those offered by 'the experts'.

Story writing 'pick and mix' 10

Here is the tenth and final collection of stimulating story writing ideas to engage child authors and enrich professional practices. As explained in 'Story writing "pick and mix" 1' (see pp. 20–21) this assortment of ideas is not attributed to a particular age phase but is offered more as a selection of suggestions for professionals to choose from and adapt in response to the writing needs of their child authors – *put an 'X' by any that you think you might try out!*

X

Story plotting: Encourage child authors to plot stories they plan to write using various graphs and charts e.g. a *line graph* to represent a story mountain, a *pie chart* to establish the content of each paragraph of the story. Visit http://tinyurl.com/7m553wc for an interesting graphing idea based on a story character's ups and downs to reveal the story shape. *Might your child authors want to create one of these?*
Story changes: Challenge child authors to write a stimulating story in response to the following 'change' ideas: • The iron that could change the colour of clothes it irons! • The road sign that could change its directions to alleviate boredom! • The mirror that could change the reflection of those who stand in front of it! See *Changes* by Browne (1997) as a useful stimulus.
Story occasions: Work with child authors to write different types of stories for different occasions e.g. *Pillow stories* (stories for bedtime), *Duvet Day stories* (stories to chill out to) or *Zippy stories* (stories for getting active to). What kinds of stories could they write for *Wedding day, Birthday, Christmas Day* or emotional days e.g. *Happy Day, Depressing Day, Angry Day* or *Exciting Day?*
'Reading is believing' story: 'Imagine that there is a girl who was born with an illness which meant that she was never able to leave the hospital. One day she asks the question: "What is it like outside?" Write a story for her that paints a wonderful picture of the world outside of the hospital to inspire the girl to get better.'
Story superhero: Introduce child authors to a new superhero: *Captain Kaloney, Space Raider of the Century. 'What does he / she look like? Which century do you think is being referred to here? How are they a "good raider"? Where do they visit in space and why? What are they the captain of?'* Oh – the story possibilities!
Story starburst: Visit http://tinyurl.com/cvlelu, offering the available PDF to child authors in an effort to introduce them to an innovative brainstorming / thought showering strategy that can be adapted for stimulating story planning.

Conclusion

...tap-tap-tap.

The tapping finally stopped.

The end.

References

Allan, T. (2008) *The Mythic Bestiary: The Illustrated Guide to the World's Most Fantastical Creatures*. London: Duncan Baird Publishers.

Allen, S. (2010) *The Inspired Writer vs. the Real Writer*. [Online.] Available at: www.parlorpress.com/pdf/allen--the-inspired-writing-vs-the-real-writer.pdf (accessed: 18 January 2015).

Altman, H. (2010) Celebrity culture: Are Americans too focused on celebrities? In *Issues for Debate in Sociology. Selections From CQ Researcher*. [Online.] Available at: www.sagepub.com/upm-data/31937_1.pdf (accessed: 1 May 2014).

Andersen, H.C. (2014) *The Little Mermaid*. Location Unknown: Hythloday Press.

Anderson, E.N. (2005) *Everyone Eats: Understanding Food and Culture*. New York: New York University Press.

Anstey, M. and Bull, G. (2009) Developing new literacies: Responding to picturebooks in multiliterate ways. In J. Evans (ed.) *Talking Beyond the Page: Reading and Responding to Picturebooks*. Abingdon: Routledge.

Appel, L. (n.d.) *How children react and what they think about having music on while writing*. [Online.] Available at: http://tinyurl.com/ocec323 (accessed: 10 December 2014).

Appelcline, K. (n.d.) Writing dynamic settings. *Skotos*. [Online.] Available at: www.skotos.net/articles/DynamicSettings.html (accessed: 7 December 2014).

Archer, J. (2014) *A Twist in the Tale*. London: Pan Books.

Armes, J. (2009) Teacher tips: Stimulate creative writing ideas with pictures. *EzineArticles*, 10 September. [Online.] Available at: http://ezinearticles.com/?Teacher-Tips---Stimulate-Creative-Writing-Ideas-With-Pictures&id=2904575 (accessed: 7 April 2014).

Babauta, L. (2008) Short stories: The art of the start. *Write To Done*. [Online.] Available at: http://writetodone.com/short-stories-the-art-of-the-start/ (accessed: 12 January 2015).

Babbage, K.J. (2010) *Extreme Writing: Discovering the Writer in Every Student*. Plymouth: Rowman & Littlefield Education.

Baddiel, D. (2014) *The Parent Agency*. London: HarperCollins Children's Books.

Balance Publishing Company (1989) *Read-Along Radio Dramas*. [Online.] Available at: www.balancepublishing.com/literary%20terms.pdf (accessed: 24 December 2014).

Barrow, M. (2013) *Ancient Egypt*. [Online.] Available at: http://resources.woodlands-junior.kent.sch.uk/homework/egypt/writing.htm (accessed: 13 October 2014).

Bartram, S. (2004) *Dougal's Deep-Sea Diary*. Woking: Templar Publishing.

Baudet, S. (2013) No conflict – No story: Creating conflict in childrens books. *LiveGuru*. [Online.] Available at: http://live.guru/articles/no-conflict-no-story-creating-conflict-in-childrens-books (accessed: 2 April 2014).

Bayne, G.K. (2015) How to write a script for a sequel. *ehow*. [Online.] Available at: www.ehow.com/how_4425212_write-script-sequel.html (accessed: 22 January 2015).

BBC (2009) *My Story. Everyone Has a Story to Tell. What's Yours? Resources: Planning Your Writing.* [Online.] Available at: http://centreforfoundationallearning.files.wordpress.com/2012/09/mystory_planning.doc (accessed: 2 June 2015).

Beaty, A. (2013) *Rosie Revere, Engineer.* New York: Abrams Books for Young Readers.

Becker, J. (2014) *7 Minimalist Lessons I've Learned From My Kids.* [Online.] Available at: http://tinyurl.com/p98kaw2 (accessed: 3 August 2014).

Belot, M., James, J. and Nolen, P. (2014) *Incentives and Children's Dietary Choices: A Field Experiment in Primary Schools.* [Online.] Available at: www.bath.ac.uk/economics/research/working-papers/2014-papers/25-14.pdf (accessed: 1 February 2015).

Bennett, C. (2014) *Dough Disco Parent Workshop.* [Online.] Available at: www.hodgehillprimary.bham.sch.uk/pdfs/pres-doughdisco.pdf (accessed: 16 February 2015).

Berkun, S. (2005) *#44 – How to learn from your mistakes.* [Online.] Available at: http://scottberkun.com/essays/44-how-to-learn-from-your-mistakes/ (accessed: 12 June 2013).

Bernays, A. and Painter, P. (1990) *What If…? Writing Exercises for Fiction Writers.* New York: HarperCollins Publishers.

BFI (2003) *Look Again! A Teaching Guide to Using Film and Television with Three- to Eleven-Year Olds.* London: *bfi* Education. [Online.] Available at: www.bfi.org.uk/sites/bfi.org.uk/files/downloads/bfi-education-look-again-teaching-guide-to-film-and-tv-2013-03.pdf (accessed: 16 January 2015).

BFI (2006) *Story Shorts 2. Using Short Films in the Primary Classroom 7+ Years. bfi* Education.

Blake, Q. (2015) *Tell Me a Picture: Adventures in Looking at Art.* London: Francis Lincoln Children's Books.

Bloom, B., Englehart, M., Furst, E., Hill, W. and Krathwohl, D. (1956) *Taxonomy of Educational Objectives: The Classification of Educational Goals. Handbook I: Cognitive Domain.* New York: Longman.

Bodenhafer, W.B. (1930) Cooley's theories of competition and conflict. *Publications of the American Sociological Association,* 25: 18–24.

Bond, M. (2003) *A Bear Called Paddington.* London: HarperCollins Children's Books.

Bowkett, S. (2010) *Developing Literacy and Creative Writing Through Storymaking: Story Strands for 7–12 Year Olds.* Maidenhead: Open University Press.

Boyce, W.T. (2012) A biology of misfortune. *Focus,* 29(1): 1–6. [Online.] Available at: www.irp.wisc.edu/publications/focus/pdfs/foc291a.pdf (accessed: 2 January 2015).

Brown Agins, D. (2006) *Maya Angelou. 'Diversity Makes for a Rich Tapestry.'* Berkeley Heights, NJ: Enslow Publishers.

Browne, A. (1997) *Changes.* London: Walker Books.

Browne, A. (2011) *Me and You.* London: Random House Children's Publishers UK.

Brownhill, S. (2013) *Getting Children Writing: Story Ideas for Children Aged 3–11.* London: Sage.

Brownhill, S. (2014) Supporting teachers' reflective practice through the use of self-reflective shapes. *Pedagogical Dialogue,* 4(10): 132–135.

Brownhill, S. (2016) *Stimulating Emerging Story Writing! Inspiring children aged 3–7.* Abingdon: Routledge.

Browning, L. (n.d.) *What Do You Mean 'Think Before I Act?' Conflict Resolution With Choices.* A Teacher Inquiry Project. Submitted as Partial Fulfillment of the Requirements For the Degree Master of Education. Southwest Texas State University, San Marcos, Texas. [Online.] Available at: www.positivediscipline.com/research/What%20Do%20You%20Mean%20Think%20Before%20I%20Act.pdf (accessed: 20 April 2014).

Buck, N.S. (2011) Parents and children in conflict: Is this the year you have resolved to stop arguing with your kids? Peaceful Parenting. *Psychology Today,* 7 January. [Online.] Available at: www.psychologytoday.com/blog/peaceful-parenting/201101/parents-children-in-conflict (accessed: 9 January 2015).

Burke, C.L. and Copenhaver, J.G. (2004) Animals as people in children's literature. *Language Arts*, 81(3): 205–213.

Burns, T. (n.d.) Conflict avoidance styles and tactics. *eHow*. [Online.] Available at: www.ehow.co.uk/info_8211130_conflict-avoidance-styles-tactics.html (accessed: 10 January 2015).

Cairney, T. (2009) Key themes in children's literature: Problem solving. *Literacy, Families and Learning*, 14 May. [Online.] Available at: http://trevorcairney.blogspot.co.uk/2009/05/key-themes-in-childrens-literature.html (accessed: 17 January 2015).

Cairney, T. (2011) Stories in a box: Stimulating language, writing and imagination. *Literacy, Families and Learning*, 20 January. [Online.] Available at: http://tinyurl.com/oyse7yv (accessed: 10 August 2014).

Calderdale and Huddersfield NHS Trust (2012) *The Narrative Activity Pack*. [Online.] Available at: http://tinyurl.com/loq4rt3 (accessed: 26 December 2014).

Cameron, L. and Besser, S. (2004) *Writing in English as an Additional Language at Key Stage 2*. Research Report RR586. London: Department for Education and Skills. [Online.] Available at: www.naldic.org.uk/Resources/NALDIC/Research%20and%20Information/Documents/RR586.pdf (accessed: 24 June 2015).

Campbell, T.A. and Hlusek, M. (2009) *Storytelling and Story Writing: 'Using a different kind of pencil'*. Research Monograph # 20, What Works? Research into Practice, The Literacy and Numeracy Secretariat. Toronto: Ontario Ministry of Education.

Cantador, I. and Conde, J.M. (n.d.) Effects of competition in education: A case study in an e-learning environment. In *Proceedings of IADIS International Conference e-Learning 2010 (E-Learning 2010)* (July). Freiburg. [Online.] Available at: http://arantxa.ii.uam.es/~cantador/doc/2010/elearning10.pdf (accessed: 1 February 2015).

Carlson Berne, E. (n.d.) 'What-if...?' Story Ideas – Story Starters. *Creative Writing Now*. [Online.] Available at: www.creative-writing-now.com/story-ideas.html (accessed: 23 December 2014).

Carroll, L. (2008) *Alice's Adventures in Wonderland*. Cathair na Mart: Evertype.

Carroll, L. (2009) *Through The Looking Glass and What Alice Found There*. Cathair na Mart: Evertype.

Carter, J. (2012) *Just Imagine: Music, Images and Text to Inspire Creative Writing*. 2nd edition. Abingdon: Routledge.

Cavazos, M. (2015) Conflict avoidance strategies. *eHow*. [Online.] Available at: www.ehow.com/list_6892527_conflict-avoidance-strategies.html (accessed: 10 January 2015).

Chen, C.-F.E. (2014) Folktales (or fairy tales). *Children's Literature*. [Online.] Available at: http://www2.nkfust.edu.tw/~emchen/CLit/folk_lit_type_folktale.htm (accessed: 7 January 2015).

Church, E.B. (2014) Why colors and shapes matter. *Little Scholastic*. [Online.] Available at: www.scholastic.com/browse/article.jsp?id=3746476 (accessed: 26 July 2014).

Cizakca, D. (n.d.) *Long Nights in Coffeehouses: The Effects of Place on Ottoman storytellers*. University of Glasgow. [Online.] Available at: www.inter-disciplinary.net/wp-content/uploads/2011/08/cizakcasppaper.pdf (accessed: 26 December 2014).

Clark, C. (2011) Setting the baseline: The National Literacy Trust's first annual survey into reading – 2010. London: National Literacy Trust. In DfE (2012) *Research Evidence on Reading for Pleasure*. [Online.] Available at: https://www.gov.uk/government/publications/research-evidence-on-reading-for-pleasure (accessed: 2 June 2015).

Cleaver, P. (2006) *Ideas for Children's Writers. A Comprehensive Resource Book of Plots, Themes, Genres, Lists, What's Hot & What's Not*. Oxford: How To Books Ltd.

Cleese, J. (2014) *So, Anyway...* London: Random House Books.

Coleman, P.T., Deutsch, M. and Marcus, E.C. (2014) *The Handbook of Conflict Resolution*. 3rd edition. San Francisco, CA: Jossey Bass.

Conklin, T. (2003) *Comprehension Cliffhanger Stories*. New York: Scholastic Professional Books.

Copeland, K. (2000) *The Decision Is Yours*. Fort Worth, TX: Kenneth Copeland Publications.

Corbett, P. (2001) *How to Teach Fiction Writing at Key Stage 2*. London: David Fulton.

Corbett, P. (2003) *How to Teach Story Writing at Key Stage 1*. London: David Fulton [reprinted 2010 by Routledge, Abingdon].

Corbett, P. (2007) *The Bumper Book of Story Telling into Writing at Key Stage 2*. Strathfield: Clown Publishing.

Corbett, P. (2008a) *Storytelling and story-making. The National Strategies: Primary*. [Online.] Available at: http://tinyurl.com/o3wewd2 (accessed: 26 September 2013).

Corbett, P. (2008b) Warning stories. *Times Educational Supplement*, 12 May. [Online.] Available at: www.tes.co.uk/article.aspx?storycode=2345072 (accessed: 20 April 2014).

Corbett, P. (2009) *Jumpstart! Storymaking Games and Activities for Ages 7–12*. Abingdon: Routledge.

Corbett, P. and Moses, B. (1991) *My Grandmother's Motorbike: Story Writing in the Primary School*. Oxford: Oxford University Press.

Cottringer, W.S. (2005) *Rectifying Mistakes*. [Online.] Available at: www.excellenceessentials.com/en/topleaders/all_articles/rectifying-mistakes_chnmsch4.html (accessed: 12 June 2013).

Creative Writing Now (2013) *Forty-Four Short Story Ideas*. [Online.] Available at: www.creative-writing-now.com/short-story-ideas.html (accessed: 30 September 2013).

Creffield, F. (n.d.) *Conflict Resolution: A Compromise for 5 Relationship Dilemmas*. [Online.] Available at: http://tinyurl.com/paqtpc7 (accessed: 31 December 2014).

Cremin, T. (2006) Creativity, uncertainty and discomfort: Teachers as writers. *Cambridge Journal of Education*, 36(3): 415–433.

Cremin, T., Goouch, K., Blakemore, L., Goff, E. and Macdonald, R. (2006) Connecting drama and writing: Seizing the moment to write. *Research in Drama in Education*, 11(3): 273–291. [Online.] Available at: http://oro.open.ac.uk/9778/1/9778.pdf (accessed: 26 April 2014).

Cremin, T., McDonald, R., Goff, E. and Blakemore, L. (2008) *Jumpstart Drama!* London: David Fulton.

Cross, G. (2009) *The Demon Headmaster*. Oxford: Oxford University Press.

Cunha, D. (2013) Compromise activities for children. *Livestrong.com*, 7 March. [Online.] Available at: www.livestrong.com/article/562082-compromise-activities-for-children/ (accessed: 31 December 2014).

Cutspec, P.A. (2006) Oral storytelling within the context of the parent–child relationship. *Talaris Research Institute*, 1(2): 1–8. [Online.] Available at: www.talaris.org/wp-content/uploads/oralstorytelling.pdf (accessed: 2 April 2015).

Dahl, R. (2007) *George's Marvellous Medicine*. London: Puffin Books.

Dargin, P. (1996) *Story Adaptation*. [Online.] Available at: www.australianstorytelling.org.au/storytelling-articles/n-s/story-adaptation-peter-dargin (accessed: 11 March 2014).

Daywalt, D. (2013) *The Day the Crayons Quit*. London: HarperCollins Children's Books.

DeNora, T. (2000) *Music in Everyday Life*. Cambridge: Cambridge University Press.

Despeaux, C. (2012) How to use misfortune to make your writing stronger. *OneWildWord.com*, 4 January. [Online.] Available at: http://onewildword.com/2012/01/04/how-to-use-misfortune-to-make-your-writing-stronger/ (accessed: 2 January 2015).

Dewan, P. (n.d.a) Introduction to children's literature classics. *Children's Literature Classics: Discover the Wonder and Magic*. [Online.] Available at: http://childliterature.net/childlit/index.html (accessed: 18 December 2014).

Dewan, P. (n.d.b) The toy genre. *Children's Literature Classics: Discover the Wonder and Magic*. [Online.] Available at: http://childliterature.net/childlit/toy/index.html (accessed: 27 September 2013).

DfE (2012) *What Is the Research Evidence on Writing? Research Report DFE-RR238*. [Online.] Available at: https://www.gov.uk/government/uploads/system/uploads/attachment_data/file/183399/DFE-RR238.pdf (accessed: 4 April 2015).

DfE (2013) *English Programmes of Study: Key Stages 1 and 2 – National Curriculum in England*. [Online.] Available at: https://www.gov.uk/government/uploads/system/uploads/attachment_data/file/335186/PRIMARY_national_curriculum_-_English_220714.pdf (accessed: 4 April 2015).

DfE (2014) *National Curriculum Assessments at Key Stage 2 in England, 2014 (Revised)*. [Online.] Available at: https://www.gov.uk/government/uploads/system/uploads/attachment_data/file/384958/SFR50_2014_Text.pdf (accessed: 4 April 2015).

DfES (2001) *Stories With Familiar Settings – Aspects of Narrative, The National Literacy Strategy*. [Online.] Available at: http://tinyurl.com/qh7olk3 (accessed: 12 April 2014).

DfES (2002) *Year 6 Planning Exemplification 2002–2003: Narrative Writing Unit*. [Online.] Available at: http://dera.ioe.ac.uk/4825/5/nls_y6t1exunits075202narr1.pdf (accessed: 15 January 2015).

DfES (2005) *Conflict and Confrontation*. 1748–2005PD5-EN. [Online.] Available at: http://dera.ioe.ac.uk/11097/2/pri_ba_conflict_cnfrnt174805.pdf (accessed: 9 January 2015).

DfES (2009) *The Crucial Role of the Early Years Practitioner in Supporting Young Writers Within a Literacy-Rich Environment*. [Online.] Available at: www.foundationyears.org.uk/wp-content/uploads/2011/11/Gateway-to-Writing-crucial-role-of-the-early-years-practitioner.pdf (accessed: 27 September 2013).

Dickens, C. (2008) *A Christmas Carol*. London: Puffin Books.

Doherty, B. (2009) *Street Child*. London: HarperCollins Children's Books.

Donnelly, L. (2013) Children as young as five suffering from depression. *The Telegraph*, 30 September. [Online.] Available at: www.telegraph.co.uk/health/healthnews/10342447/Children-as-young-as-five-suffering-from-depression.html (accessed: 21 April 2014).

du Maurier, D. (2004) *The Birds and Other Stories*. London: Virago Press.

Durand, P. (2007) *The Quest Plot: How to Create a Quest Plot for Your Story*. [Online.] Available at: http://tinyurl.com/nftdpmv (accessed: 5 June 2015).

Dutta, S. (2003) A fly in the sweetshop. In N. Menon (ed.) *Indian Tales and Folk Tales*. New Delhi: Children's Book Trust, pp. 26–31. [Online.] Available at: http://tinyurl.com/qa2s57o (accessed: 23 December 2014).

Elks, E. and McLachlan, H. (2014) *Colourful Stories*. [Online.] Available at: https://elklantraining.worldsecuresystems.com/resources/colourful-stories (accessed: 8 June 2015).

Emery, D.W. (1996) Helping readers comprehend stories from the characters' perspectives. *The Reading Teacher*, 49(7): 534–541.

EmpoweringWriters.com (2004) *Narrative Writing*. [Online.] Available at: http://empoweringwriters.ca/improving-student-writing/teaching-narrative-writing/introduction-narrative-writing/feelings-look-like/ (accessed: 10 December 2014).

English, C. and Broadhead, P. (2004) Theatre and open-ended play in the early years – combining to promote opportunities for creativity. *Topic*, 32: 13–18. [Online.] Available at: www.nfer.ac.uk/nfer/pre_pdf_files/04_32_02.pdf (accessed: 12 June 2015).

Epstein, P. (2014) How to develop writing in young children. *eHow*. [Online.] Available at: www.ehow.com/how_7348833_develop-writing-young-children.html (accessed: 16 October 2014).

Evans, B. (2011) Bullying: Can it begin in preschool? *Extensions*, 25(3): 1–6. [Online.] Available at: www.highscope.org/file/NewsandInformation/Extensions/ExtVol25No3_low.pdf (accessed: 8 January 2015).

Evans, J. (2013) Using nursery rhymes, jingles, songs and poems as a way into writing. In J. Evans (ed.) *The Writing Classroom: Aspects of Writing and the Primary Child, 3–11*. Abingdon: Routledge, pp. 8–18.

Everson, B. (1991) Vygotsky and the teaching of writing. *The Quarterly*, 13(3): 8–11. [Online.] Available at: http://tinyurl.com/onx6av8 (accessed: 15 January 2015).

Fassler, J. (2013) Why Stephen King spends 'months and even years' writing opening sentences. *The Atlantic*, 23 July. [Online.] Available at: www.theatlantic.com/entertainment/archive/2013/07/why-stephen-king-spends-months-and-even-years-writing-opening-sentences/278043/ (accessed: 4 January 2014).

Fine, A. (2009) *The Diary of a Killer Cat*. London: Puffin.

Foreman, M. (2009) *Wonder Goal*. London: Anderson Press.

Foster, J. (2005) *Word Whirls and Other Shape Poems*. Oxford: Oxford University Press.

Foster, J. (2014) *Let's Write: Activities to Develop Writing Skills for 7–11 Year Olds*. London: David Fulton.

Fox, L. and Lentini, R.H. (2006) Teaching children a vocabulary for emotions. *Beyond the Journal*. Young Children on the Web, November. [Online.] Available at: www.naeyc.org/files/yc/file/200611/BTJFoxSupplementalActivities.pdf (accessed: 12 June 2013).

Frank, A. (2009) *The Diary of a Young Girl*. London: Puffin Classics.

Frazier, B. (2001) Helping children build a conscience. *The Successful Parent*, 19 July. [Online.] Available at: www.thesuccessfulparent.com/moral-development/helping-children-build-a-conscience (accessed: 21 April 2014).

Freeman, S.W. (2010) 6 ways to hook your readers from the very first line. *Write It Sideways*. [Online.] Available at: http://writeitsideways.com/6-ways-to-hook-your-readers-from-the-very-first-line/ (accessed: 23 January 2015).

French, F. (1995) *Snow White in New York*. Oxford: Oxford University Press.

Gall, C. (2013) *Awesome Dawson*. New York: Little, Brown Books for Young Readers.

Ganeri, A. (2015) *Remembering the Dead Around the World*. Basingstoke: Raintree.

Garber, S. (2002) *Memorable Characters...Magnificent Stories*. New York: Scholastic Professional Books.

Garrett, J. (1996) Introduction. In B. Preiss (ed.) *The Best Children's Books in the World: A Treasury of Illustrated Stories*. New York: Abrams, pp. 7–9.

Gerngross, G. and Puchta, H. (1996) *Do and Understand: 50 Action Stories for Young Learners*. Harlow: Longman. [Online.] Available at: www.vidyaonline.net/dl/dolang.pdf (accessed: 15 January 2015).

Gleitzman, M. (2008) *Give Peas a Chance*. London: Puffin Books.

Goldman, K. (1993) Seniors get little respect on Madison Avenue. *Wall Street Journal*, 20 September, p. B4.

Gottman, J. (n.d.) *Predicting Divorce – John Gottman*. [Online.] Available at: http://isoulseek.com/sitebranches/relationskills/articles/6signs.pdf (accessed: 10 January 2015).

Graham, S. and Perin, D. (2007) *Writing Next: Effective strategies to improve writing of adolescents in middle and high schools – A report to the Carnegie Corporation of New York*. Washington, DC: Alliance for Excellent Education. In General Teaching Council for England (GTC) (2008) *Research for Teachers: Strategies for Improving Pupils' Writing Skills*. [Online.] Available at: http://tinyurl.com/73p4j7r (accessed: 29 December 2014).

Grainger, T. (2005) Teachers as writers: Learning together. *English in Education*, 39(1): 75–87. [Online.] Available at: http://oro.open.ac.uk/16431/2/29CFFB51.pdf (accessed: 30 March 2015).

Graves, A., Semmel, M. and Gerber, M. (1994) The effects of story prompts on the narrative production of students with and without learning disabilities. *Learning Disability Quarterly*, 17(2): 154–164.

Gray, K. (2014) *Daisy and the Trouble with Sports Day*. London: Red Fox.

Grossman, J. (2013) What are Snapchat stories? *Information Space*, 10 October. [Online.] Available at: http://infospace.ischool.syr.edu/2013/10/10/what-are-snapchat-stories/ (accessed 23 December 2014).

Hadley-Garcia, G. (2013) 'Extreme' characters fuel the plot of 'The Master'. *The Japan Times*, 5 April. [Online.] Available at: www.japantimes.co.jp/culture/2013/04/05/films/extreme-characters-fuel-the-plot-of-the-master/#.Uba5oL5waM8 (accessed: 11 June 2013).

Haloin, M., Jameson, G., Piccolo, J. and Oosterveen, K. (2005) Genre characteristics. In R. Routman (2005) *Writing Essentials*. Portsmouth, NH: Heinemann. [Online.] Available at: www.ux1.eiu.edu/~cfder/GenreCharacteristicsChart.pdf (accessed: 30 December 2014).

Hardy, J. (2014) An age-old question: How do you show a character's age? *Janice Hardy's Fiction University*, 12 February. [Online.] Available at: http://blog.janicehardy.com/2014/02/an-age-old-question-how-do-you-show.html (accessed: 30 November 2014).

Harrington, A. (2015) *Creative Writing for Kids: Vol 1 & 2*. New edition. Available via Lulu.com.

Hawkinge Primary School (2013) *Bang!* Amazon CreateSpace Independent Publishing Platform.

Helsley, D. (2011) *The Day No One Played Together: A Story About Compromise*. Milwaukee, WI: Mirror Publishing.

Hickman, S. (2014) What is an internal conflict? *eHow*. [Online.] Available at: www.ehow.com/about_5598083_internal-conflict_.html (accessed: 21 April 2014).

Hodgins, J. (2001) *A Passion for Narrative: A Guide for Writing Fiction*. Revised edition. Toronto: McClelland & Stewart Ltd.

Holdich, C.E. and Chung, P.W.H. (2003) A 'computer tutor' to assist children develop their narrative writing skills: Conferencing with HARRY. *International Journal of Human-Computer Studies*, 59(5): 631–669.

Hopwood-Stephens, I. (2013) *Learning on Your Doorstep: Stimulating Writing Through Creative Play Outdoors for Ages 5–9*. Abingdon: Routledge.

Horn, C.V. (n.d.) *Elements of Literature: Point of View*. [Online.] Available at: www.nps.gov/mora/forteachers/upload/background-elements-of-literature_sr.pdf (accessed: 29 December 2014).

Huff, K.J. (2000) *Storytelling With Puppets, Props, and Playful Tales*. Dunstable: Brilliant Publications.

Hughes, T. (2005) *The Iron Man: A Children's Story in Five Nights*. London: Faber and Faber.

Ings, R. (2009) *Writing Is Primary*. [Online.] Available at: http://tinyurl.com/ngjmxty (accessed: 8 April 2015).

Irvine, J. (2005) *Easy-To-Make Pop-Ups*. Mineola, NY: Dover Publications.

Isenberg, J.P. and Jalongo, M.R. (2010) *Types of Children's Conflicts*. [Online.] Available at: www.education.com/reference/article/types-childrens-conflicts/ (accessed: 10 January 2015).

James, S. (2004) *Baby Brains: The Smartest Baby in the Whole World*. London: Walker Books.

Jasper, M. (2006) *Professional Development, Reflection and Decision-Making*. Oxford: Blackwell Publishing.

Jeffers, O. (2005) *Lost and Found*. London: Philomel Books.

Jeffers, O. (2011) *The Heart and the Bottle*. London: HarperCollins Children's Books.

Johns, L.C. (2004) *The Writing Coach*. Clifton Park, NY: Delmar Learning.

Johnson, D. (2010) *Love: Bondage or Liberation?* London: Karnac Books Ltd.

Jones, A. (2012) *Action Stories for Children*. [Online.] Available at: www.ihes.com/bcn/tt/eltconf/12/action_stories_with_children.pdf (accessed: 15 January 2015).

Jones, L. (2014) The role weather played on D-Day. *9 WAFB*, 4 July. [Online.] Available at: www.wafb.com/story/25711519/the-role-weather-played-on-d-day (accessed: 31 July 2014).

Jones, S.A. and Jones, A.C. (2008) *Creative Story Writing (Levels 3–6, Ages 9–14)*. New Haw: Guinea Pig Education.

Jones, V.S.V. (2006) *Aesop's Fables*. London: Collector's Library.

Jose, P.E. and Brewer, W.F. (1983) *The Development of Story Liking: Character Identification, Suspense and Outcome Resolution*. Technical Report No. 291, University of Illinois. [Online.] Available at: https://www.ideals.illinois.edu/bitstream/handle/2142/17668/ctrstreadtechrepv01983i00291_opt.pdf?sequence=1 (accessed: 26 December 2014).

Keene, N. (2009) *Identity Theft*. New York: Simon & Schuster Children's Publishing Division.

Kellaher, K. (1999) *101 Picture Prompts to Spark Super Writing Reproducible Photographs, Cartoons & Art Masterpieces to Intrigue, Amuse & Inspire Every Writer in Your Class!* New

York: Scholastic, Inc. [Online.] Available at: http://tinyurl.com/q8sqvtm (accessed: 25 July 2014).

Kemp, J. and Walters, C. (2003) *Travel Games*. London: Hamlyn.

Kendell, J. (2004) *SAT Attack Reading/Writing: Teachers Guide*. Oxford: Harcourt Education.

KidsHealth in the Classroom (2006) *Conflict Resolution*. [Online.] Available at: http://kidshealth.org/classroom/3to5/personal/growing/conflict_resolution.pdf (accessed: 9 January 2015).

King-Smith, D. (2013) *Billy the Bird*. London: Young Corgi Books.

Kinney, J. (2007) *Diary of a Wimpy Kid*. London: Puffin.

Kipling, R. (2007) *The Jungle Book*. Oxford: Oxford University Press.

Kipling, R. and Davis, L. (1992) *Rikki-Tikki-Tavi*. San Diego CA: Harcourt Children's Books.

Kitamura, S. (2009) *Millie's Marvellous Hat*. London: Anderson Press.

Klein, A. (2004) *Ready, Freddy! Homework Hassles*. New York: Scholastic Inc.

Klems, B. (2012) The 7 rules of picking names for fictional characters. *Writer's Digest*, 28 August. [Online.] Available at: www.writersdigest.com/online-editor/the-7-rules-of-picking-names-for-fictional-characters (accessed: 24 March 2015).

Knapton, S. (2014) Reading fairy stories to children is harmful, says Richard Dawkins. *The Telegraph*, 4 June. [Online.] Available at: www.telegraph.co.uk/news/science/science-news/10875912/Reading-fairy-stories-to-children-is-harmful-says-Richard-Dawkins.html (accessed: 7 January 2015).

Koran, S. (2014) *Cinderella's Son and Snow White's Daughter: The Untold Sequels to the Fairy Tales*. Tel-Aviv: Contento de Semrik.

Lange, A. (n.d.) 10 steps to creating realistic fantasy animals. *Elfwood*. [Online.] Available at: www.elfwood.com/tutorial/1d8952ad-56c9-b836-dea8-2904e4991868/10-steps-to-creating-realistic-fantasy-animals (accessed: 13 April 2015).

Laniyan-Amoako, O. (2010) Black publisher fights to bring more books to black and ethnic minority readers. *Caribbean Book Blog*, 6 March. [Online.] Available at: https://caribbeanbookblog.wordpress.com/2010/03/06/black-publisher-fights-to-bring-more-books-to-black-and-ethnic-minority-readers/ (accessed: 30 November 2014).

Lansky, B. (2015) How to write a *Girls to the Rescue* story. *FictionTeacher.com*. [Online.] Available at: www.fictionteachers.com/fictionclass/gtrhowto.html (accessed: 17 January 2015).

Lawrence, M. (2001) *The Toilet of Doom*. London: Orchard Books.

Lee, R.L. Jr and Fraser, A.B. (2001) *The Rainbow Bridge: Rainbows in Art, Myth and Science*. New York: Pennsylvania State University Press and SPIE Press.

Leochko, D. (2000) *25 Quick Mini-Lessons to Teach Narrative Writing*. New York: Scholastic Inc.

Leonard, E. (2010) *10 Rules of Writing*. London: Weidenfeld & Nicolson.

Levine, K. (2003) *Hana's Suitcase*. Park Ridge, IL: Albert Whitman & Company.

LifeCare (2011) *Conflict Resolution*. [Online.] Available at: www.wfm.noaa.gov/workplace/EmotionalIntell_Handout_4.pdf (accessed: 24 January 2015).

Lloyd, J., Mitchinson, J. and Harkin, J. (2014) *1,411 QI Facts to Knock You Sideways*. London: Faber & Faber.

London, J. (2013) *Love of Life*. Amazon CreateSpace Independent Publishing Platform.

Lopez, L. (n.d.) Fantastical Beasts. *The J. Paul Getty Museum*. [Online.] Available at: www.getty.edu/education/teachers/classroom_resources/curricula/arts_lang_arts/a_la_lesson35.html (accessed: 26 May 2014).

Lopresti, A. (2008) *Fantastical Creatures Field Guide: How to Hunt Them Down and Draw Them Where They Live*. New York: Watson-Guptill.

Lou, E. (2011) The 6 weirdest dangers of space travel. *Cracked*, 23 April. [Online.] Available at: www.cracked.com/article_19158_the-6-weirdest-dangers-space-travel.html (accessed: 26 March 2015).

Lucke, M. (1999) *Schaum's Quick Guide to Writing Great Short Stories*. New York: McGraw Hill. [Online.] Available at: http://tinyurl.com/n34ps8f (accessed: 8 September 2014).

Lyness, D'A. (2013) Fears and phobias. *TeensHealth*, May. [Online.] Available at: http://kidshealth.org/teen/cancer_center/feelings/phobias.html (accessed: 5 December 2014).

Malindine, D. (2013) *Tutor Master Helps You Write Stories: Book Two*. Middlesex: Tutor Master Services.

Manohar, U. (2011) What are the most exciting jobs in the world. *Buzzle*, 19 December. [Online.] Available at: www.buzzle.com/articles/what-are-the-most-exciting-jobs-in-the-world.html (accessed: 30 November 2014).

Martin, L.J. (2011) Themes in children's fiction. *Literature for Kids*. [Online.] Available at: www.literature4kids.com/themes-in-childrens-fiction (accessed: 14 December 2014).

Marylebone Cricket Club and Chance to Shine (2014) *It's only a game? Competition in school sport under threat*. 22 April. [Online.] Available at: http://tinyurl.com/poolsd3 (accessed: 3 August 2014).

Matthews, A. (2003) *A Midsummer Night's Dream: A Shakespeare Story*. London: Orchard Books.

Mattice, C. (2010) *One Word Writing Prompts*. [Online.] Available at: http://beingawriter.typepad.com/being-a-writer/2010/05/one-word-writing-prompts.html (accessed: 29 September 2013).

Maynard, T. (2002) *Boys and Literacy: Exploring the Issues*. London: RoutledgeFalmer.

Maynes, N. and Julien-Schultz, L. (2011) The impact of visual frameworks on teacher candidates' professional reflection. *LEARNing Landscapes*, 5(1): 193–210.

McCarthy, T. (1998) *Narrative Writing*. New York: Scholastic.

Miller, S. and Pennycuff, L. (2008) The power of story: Using storytelling to improve literacy learning. *Journal of Cross-Disciplinary Perspectives in Education*, 1(1): 36–43. [Online.] Available at: http://jcpe.wmwikis.net/file/view/miller.pdf (accessed: 14 April 2015).

Mills, J.C. (2003) *Gentle Willow: A Story for Children about Dying*. 2nd edition. Washington DC: Magination Press.

Misra, A. and R, N. (2012) Conflicts with the supernatural. *The Hindu*, 26 June. [Online.] Available at: http://tinyurl.com/opyc85r (accessed: 7 January 2015).

Mitchelhill, J. (2007) *Storm Runners*. London: Anderson Press.

Mohr, K.A.J. (1993) Metamessages and problem-solving perspectives in children's literature. *Reading Horizons*, 33(4): 341–346.

Montgomery, R.A. (2006) *Choose Your Own Adventure: Box Set 1*. Waitsfield, VT: Chooseco.

Moore, J. (2005) *Teaching Sentence Structure to Primary Writers*. [Online.] Available at: www.scribd.com/doc/69665814/Teaching-Sentence-Structure-Part-One#scribd (accessed: 2 June 2015).

Morgan, G. (2006) *Space Poems*. London: Macmillan Children's Books.

Morpurgo, M. (2009) *I Believe in Unicorns*. [Online.] Available at: http://tinyurl.com/kxuvmq9 (accessed: 8 September 2014).

Morris, R. (1993) Sentence strips. *Writing Notebook: Visions for Learning*, 11(1): 35–38.

Morris, R. (2013) Music tells me stories – the undercover soundtrack. *Writers & Artists: The Insider Guide to the Media*, 16 July. [Online.] Available at: https://www.writersandartists.co.uk/2013/07/music-tells-me-stories-the-undercover-soundtrack-by-roz-morris (accessed: 5 April 2014).

MPS (2011) *Avoiding Easy Mistakes: Five Medicolegal Hazards for Junior Doctors*. London: Medical Protection Society.

Muntean, M. (2006) *Do Not Open This Book*. New York: Scholastic Press.

Myers, T.J. (2014) *Rude Dude's Book of Food*. Sanger, CA: Familius LLC.

National Literacy Trust (n.d.a) *Story Boxes*. [Online.] Available at: www.literacytrust.org.uk/assets/0000/3211/Story_box_guide.pdf (accessed: 3 May 2014).

National Literacy Trust (n.d.b) *Story Sacks*. [Online.] Available at: www.literacytrust.org.uk/assets/0000/3210/Story_sack_guide.pdf (accessed: 7 September 2014).

Nesbit, E. (2012) *The Book of Dragons*. USA: Renaissance Classics.

Nesbit, E. (2013) *The Railway Children*. London: Scholastic Classics.

Neuburger, E.K. (2012) *Show Me A Story: 40 Craft Projects and Activities to Spark Children's Storytelling*. North Adams, MA: Storey Publishing.

Newcombe, R. (2013) Learning about vehicles and transport. *Early Childhood Education*, 7 August. [Online.] Available at: www.earlychildhoodeducation.co.uk/learning-about-vehicles-transport.html (accessed: 3 May 2014).

Ngo, K. (2014) Life lessons. *MotivationalWellBeing.com* [Online.] Available at: www.motivationalwellbeing.com/life-lessons.html (accessed: 3 August 2014).

O'Sullivan, J. (2012) *Bizarre Weather*. Watertown, MA: Imagine Publishing.

OECD (2013) *Country Note: United Kingdom – Results from PISA 2012*. [Online.] Available at: www.oecd.org/unitedkingdom/PISA-2012-results-UK.pdf (accessed: 5 April 2015).

OFSTED (2009) *English at the Crossroads: An Evaluation of English in Primary and Secondary Schools, 2005/08*. [Online.] Available at: http://dera.ioe.ac.uk/298/1/English%20at%20the%20crossroads.pdf (accessed: 5 April 2015).

OFSTED (2014) *The Report of Her Majesty's Chief Inspector of Education, Children's Services and Skills 2013/14: Schools*. [Online.] Available at: https://www.gov.uk/government/uploads/system/uploads/attachment_data/file/384707/Ofsted_Annual_Report_201314_Schools.pdf (accessed: 3 April 2015)

Oh My Disney (2013) *What We Learned From Toy Story*. 23 March. [Online.] Available at: http://tinyurl.com/osw3apg (accessed: 3 August 2014).

ONS (2012) *Families and Households, 2012*. [Online.] Available at: www.ons.gov.uk/ons/dcp171778_284823.pdf (accessed: 24 July 2014).

Paradise, J.L. (2007) *An analysis of improving student performance through the use of registered therapy dogs serving as motivators for reluctant readers*. Doctoral dissertation. [Online.] Available at: http://etd.fcla.edu/CF/CFE0001561/Paradise_Julie_L_200705_Ed.D.pdf (accessed: 31 March 2015).

Parlakian, R. and Lerner, C. (2010) Beyond Twinkle, Twinkle: Using music with infants and toddlers. *Young Children*, March, 14–19. [Online.] Available at: www.naeyc.org/content/music (accessed: 21 January 2015).

Pastis, S. (2014) *Timmy Failure: We Meet Again*. Somerville, MA: Candlewick Press.

Paton, G. (2012) Parents 'shun bedtime reading' in favour of TV. *The Telegraph*, 19 October. [Online.] Available at: www.telegraph.co.uk/education/educationnews/9617868/Parents-shun-bedtime-reading-in-favour-of-TV.html (accessed: 2 April 2015).

Paton, G. (2014) Films and computer games 'boost children's vocabulary'. *The Telegraph*, 28 May. [Online.] Available at: www.telegraph.co.uk/education/educationnews/10860747/Films-and-computer-games-boost-childrens-vocabulary.html (accessed: 16 January 2015).

Pattison, D. (2010) *12 Ways to Start a Novel*. 10 March. [Online.] Available at: www.darcypattison.com/revision/opening-lines/ (accessed: 12 January 2015).

Pearce, P. (2008) *Tom's Midnight Garden*. Oxford: Oxford University Press.

Peat, A. (2002) *Improving Story Writing at Key Stages 1 & 2*. Oxford: Nash Pollock Publishing.

Peat, A. (2010a) *Beyond 'Happily Ever After': Improving the Ending of Narrative Texts*. [Online.] Available at: www.alanpeat.com/resources/ending.html (accessed: 6 December 2014).

Peat, A. (2010b) *Improving Narrative Openings: An Explicit Teaching Approach*. [Online.] Available at: www.alanpeat.com/resources/openings.html (accessed: 4 January 2014).

Peha, S. (2003a) *The Five Facts of Fiction*. [Online.] Available at: www.ttms.org/PDFs/10%20Five%20Facts%20of%20Fiction%20v001%20(Full).pdf (accessed: 29 December 2014).

Peha, S. (2003b) *The Writing Teacher's Strategy Guide*. [Online.] Available at: www.ttms.org/PDFs/01%20Writing%20Strategy%20Guide%20v001%20(Full).pdf (accessed: 3 January 2015).

Petrick, J.F. (2002) An examination of golf vacationers' novelty. *Annals of Tourism Research*, 29(2): 384–400.

Pett, M. and Rubinstein, G. (2012) *The Girl Who Never Made Mistakes*. Illinois: Sourcebooks, Jaberwocky.

Post-News Educational Services (n.d.) *Creating a Classroom Newspaper*. [Online.] Available at: http://tinyurl.com/pt8287n (accessed: 20 January 2015).

Powell, J. (2010) *Adventure Stories for Ages 9–11*. London: Scholastic.

Pratchett, T. (2013) *Johnny and the Dead*. London: Corgi.

Pullman, P. (2004) *The Firework-Maker's Daughter*. London: Corgi Yearling Books.

Pullman, P. (2012) *Grimm Tales: For Young and Old*. London: Penguin Classics.

Quay, E. (2006) *Characters: Animal or Human?* [Online.] Available at: www.emmaquay.com/Characters%20-%20Animal%20or%20Human.pdf (accessed: 28 December 2013).

Rees, F. (ed.) *The Writing Repertoire: Developing Writing at Key Stage Two*. Slough: National Foundation for Educational Research.

Renner, A. (n.d.) 7 ways learning to compromise improves all your relationships. *Lifehack.org*. [Online.] Available at: http://tinyurl.com/qxlpyky (accessed: 27 June 2015).

Ribena Plus (2012) The role of toys in play (Chapter 3). In *The Ribena Plus Play Report*. [Online.] Available at: www.ribena.co.uk/download/Ribena_Plus_Play_Report_Ch3.pdf (accessed: 23 June 2013).

Richardson, J. (1995) Avoidance as an active mode of conflict resolution. *Team Performance Management: An International Journal*, 1(4): 19–25.

Rinzler, A. (2011) Grand finales: Tips for writing great endings. *The Book Deal*, 31 December. [Online.] Available at: www.alanrinzler.com/blog/2011/12/31/grand-finales-tips-for-writing-great-endings/ (accessed: 3 January 2015).

Robinson, H. (2005) *Mixed Up Fairy Tales*. London: Hodder Children's Books.

Roddy, L. (2003) *How to Write a Story: A Step-by-Step Method for Understanding and Teaching Basic Story Writing Techniques*. Atascadero, CA: Institute for Excellence in Writing, Inc. [Online.] Available at: www.writing-edu.com/writing/PDF%20samples/HWS_sample.pdf (accessed: 5 December 2014).

Rodgers, M. (2003) *Freaky Friday*. New York: Avon Books.

Rojas-Drummond, S.M., Albarràn, C.D. and Littleton, K. (2008) Collaboration, creativity and the co-construction of oral and written texts. *Thinking Skills and Creativity*, 3(3): 177–191.

Rose, J. (2006) The power of color in writing. *EzineArticles*, 17 April. [Online.] Available at: http://ezinearticles.com/?The-Power-of-Color-in-Writing&id=180313 (accessed: 26 July 2014).

Rosen, M. (1997) *We're Going On A Bear Hunt*. London: Walker Books.

Rosen, M. (2011) *Michael Rosen's Sad Book*. London: Walker Books.

Ross, A. (2010) *Nutrition and Its Effects on Academic Performance: How Can Our Schools Improve?* [Online.] Available at: www.nmu.edu/sites/DrupalEducation/files/UserFiles/Files/Pre-Drupal/SiteSections/Students/GradPapers/Projects/Ross_Amy_MP.pdf (accessed: 25 February 2015).

Rowling, J.K. (2001) *Fantastic Beasts and Where To Find Them*. London: Bloomsbury Publishing.

Rowling, J.K. (2004) *Harry Potter and the Goblet of Fire*. London: Bloomsbury Publishing.

Rowling, J.K. (2007) *Harry Potter and the Deathly Hallows*. London: Bloomsbury Publishing.

Rubin, J. (2012) *Conflicts With Ourselves: Lessons from Charlie Brown*. 8 December. [Online.] Available at: http://drjeffreyrubin.wordpress.com/2012/12/08/conflicts-with-ourselves-lessons-from-charlie-brown/ (accessed: 21 April 2014).

Rumseya, I. and Ballarda, K.D. (1985) Teaching self-management strategies for independent story writing to children with classroom behaviour difficulties. *Educational Psychology: An International Journal of Experimental Educational Psychology*, 5(2): 147–157.

Sambuchino, C. (2013) The worst ways to begin your novel: Advice from literary agents. *TheWriteLife*, 6 August. [Online.] Available at: http://thewritelife.com/the-worst-ways-to-begin-your-novel-advice-from-literary-agents/#RQjp2k:pqL (accessed: 3 January 2015).

Santoso, A. (2009) 7 brilliant ideas scribbled on cocktail napkins and toilet papers. *Neatorama*, 5 March. [Online.] Available at: www.neatorama.com/2009/03/05/7-brilliant-ideas-scribbled-on-cocktail-napkins-and-toilet-papers/ (accessed: 30 November 2014).

Saunders, M., Lewis, P. and Thornhill, A. (2009) *Research Methods for Business Students*. 5th edition. Harlow: Pearson Education.

Schneider, J.J. and Jackson, S.A.W. (2000) Process drama: A special space and place for writing. *The Reading Teacher*, 54(1): 38–51.

Scieszka, J. (1991) *The Frog Prince, Continued*. London: Viking.

Selznick, R. (2012) *School Struggles: A Guide to Your Shut Down Learner's Success*. Boulder, CO: Sentiant Publications.

Sharp, J. (2000) *Making Fairies and Fantastical Creatures: How to Weave and Carve in Wool and Chenille*. Lewes: Guild of Master Craftsman Publications Ltd.

Shaw, R. (2007) *How to Write Wonderful Stories (Junior Primary)*. Hillarys, W. Australia: Intelligent Australia Productions. [Online.] Available at: https://australianteacher.files.wordpress.com/2011/01/how-to-write-wonderful-stories-junior-primary.pdf (accessed: 5 April 2015).

Shaw, R. (2008) *1001 Brilliant Writing Ideas. Teaching Inspirational Story-Writing for All Ages*. Abingdon: Routledge.

Shipton, J. (1999) *What If?* London: Macmillan Children's Books.

Silvey, A. (ed.) (1995) *Children's Books and Their Creators*. New York: Houghton Mifflin Company.

Simmonds, P. (2014) *Baker Cat*. London: Red Fox Books.

Singleton, R.S. and Conrad, J.A. (2000) *Filmmaker's dictionary*. 2nd edition. Ed. J.W. Healy. Hollywood, CA: Lone Eagle Publishing Company.

Sipe, L.R. (1993) Using transformations of traditional stories: Making the reading–writing connection. *The Reading Teacher*, 47(1): 18–26. [Online.] Available at: http://tinyurl.com/m8m4ok2 (accessed: 22 January 2015).

Smith, F. (1982) *Writing and the Writer*. New York: Holt, Rinehart and Winston.

Smith, J. (2012) *I Am Not a Loser*. London: Jelly Pie (Egmont).

Smith, M., Segal, R. and Segal, J. (2014) Phobias and fears: Symptoms, treatment, and self-help for phobias and fears. *Helpguide.org*, December. [Online.] Available at: www.helpguide.org/articles/anxiety/phobias-and-fears.htm (accessed: 5 December 2014).

Snicket, L. (1999) *The Bad Beginning*. New York: HarperCollins Children's Books.

Snyder, D. (2007) *100-Whats of Creativity*. [Online.] Available at: www.game-changer.net/2009/05/05/100-what-if-questions-ebook-to-spark-your-creativity/ (accessed: 20 December 2014).

Soar Higher (2006) *SOAR Stories*. [Online.] Available at: www.soarhigheraspen.com/docs/SOAR_Stories.pdf (accessed: 5 December 2014).

Stevens, J. and Kraneveld, S. (2013) *Colourful Stories: Exploring the Transformative Potential of Colour Culture in a Northumbrian Mining Town*. [Online.] Available at: http://nrl.northumbria.ac.uk/12634/ (accessed: 26 July 2014).

Stewart, A.-M. (2008) *The Confidence Booster*. [Online.] Available at: www.tools-for-abundance.com/support-files/confidencebooster.pdf (accessed: 19 January 2015).

Stoker, B. (1993) *Dracula*. Ware: Wordsworth Editions Limited.

Stott, J.C. (1994) Making stories mean; making meaning from stories: The value of literature for children. *Children's Literature in Education*, December, 25: 243–253.

Strauss, L.L. (2010) *Drop Everything and Write! An Easy Breezy Guide for Kids Who Want to Write a Story*. Sausalito, CA: E & E Publishing.

Sunderland, M. (2001) *Helping Children Who Bottle Up Their Feelings: A Guidebook*. Milton Keynes: Speechmark Publishing Ltd.

Tamburrini, J., Willig, J. and Butler, C. (1984) Children's conceptions of writing. In H. Cowie (ed.) *The Development of Children's Creative Writing*. London: Croom Helm, pp. 188–189.

Taylor, M.A. (2010) *The Monster Chronicles: The role of children's stories featuring monsters in managing childhood fears and promoting empowerment*. Dissertation, Queensland University of Technology. [Online.] Available at: http://eprints.qut.edu.au/37305/1/Michelle_Taylor_Thesis.pdf (accessed: 7 January 2015).

Teacher Support Force (2011) Strategies for teaching writing should include school wide events. *Teacher Support Force*. [Online.] Available at: www.teacher-support-force.com/strategies-for-teaching-writing.html (accessed: 16 October 2014).

Temean, K. (2010) Adding an ethnic character to your story. *Writing and Illustrating*, 25 October. [Online.] Available at: http://kathytemean.wordpress.com/2010/10/25/adding-an-ethnic-minority-character-to-your-story/ (accessed: 30 November 2014).

The J. Paul Getty Trust (n.d.) Telling stories in art. *The J. Paul Getty Museum*. [Online.] Available at: www.getty.edu/education/teachers/classroom_resources/curricula/stories/index.html (accessed: 8 December 2014).

The National Gallery (2015) *Take One Picture*. [Online.] Available at www.takeonepicture.org/index.html (accessed: 31 March 2015).

The Open University (2014) Writing what you know. *OpenLearn*. [Online.] Available at: www.open.edu/openlearn/history-the-arts/culture/literature-and-creative-writing/creative-writing/writing-what-you-know/content-section-3.1 (accessed: 23 December 2014).

Thomas, D. (2013) *Jungle Tangle*. Cork: Mercier Press.

Time4Writing (2011) *Writing Basics → Ending with a Cliffhanger. Level: Middle School*. [Online.] Available at: http://tinyurl.com/mlnp9hh (accessed: 19 January 2015).

Tobias, R.B. (2012) *20 Master Plots And How to Build Them*. 3rd edition. Cincinnati, OH: Writer's Digest Books.

Tocher, T. (2015) How to write a sports story. *FictionTeachers.com*. [Online.] Available at: www.fictionteachers.com/fictionclass/sportshowto.html (accessed: 17 January 2015).

Tower Hamlets EMA Team in collaboration with Tower Hamlets teachers (2009) *Progression in Language Structures*. [Online.] Available at: www.communicationacrosscultures.com/82-home/160-progression-in-language-structures (accessed: 3 April 2015).

TRUCE (2009–2010) *Toys, Play & Young Children: Action Guide*. [Online.] Available at: www.truceteachers.org/toyguides/T_Guide_web_09.pdf (accessed: 27 September 2013).

Tucker, J. (2013) *Return To Life: Extraordinary Cases of Children Who Remember Past Lives*. New York: St Martin's Press.

Twain, M. (2009) *The Adventures of Huckleberry Finn*. Oxford: Oxford University Press.

Uchiyama, K. (2006) *English Verb Tenses: An Informal but Extensive Reference for ESL Students, the Good Folks Who Teach Them, the Idly Curious, and the Linguistically Perplexed*. [Online.] Available at: www.chabotcollege.edu/languagearts/esl/verb%20tense%20book--pdf.pdf (accessed: 28 June 2015).

Unicef (n.d.) *Child Well-Being in the UK, Spain and Sweden: The Role of Inequality and Materialism*. [Online.] Available at: www.unicef.org.uk/Documents/Publications/UNICEFIpsosMori_childwellbeing_reportsummary.pdf (accessed: 30 August 2014).

Vandergrift, K.E. (1997) *Children Writing & Publishing*. 15 April. [Online.] Available at: http://comminfo.rutgers.edu/professional-development/childlit/childpublishing.html (accessed: 27 April 2014).

Verhoeff, T. (1997) *The Role of Competitions in Education*. November. [Online.] Available at: http://olympiads.win.tue.nl/ioi/ioi97/ffutwrld/competit.pdf (accessed: 5 August 2014).

Vertsman, M. (2014) Around the World in 80+ Children's Books. *New York Public Library*, 22 July. [Online.] Available at: www.nypl.org/blog/2014/07/22/around-world-childrens-books (accessed: 11 January 2014).

VIA University College (2013) *Animation as a Learning Tool*. [Online.] Available at: www. viauc.com/schools-faculties/faculty-of-education-and-social-studies/Documents/exchange-programmes/Animation-as-a-Learning-Tool.pdf (accessed: 16 January 2015).

Village Hat Shop (2015) *Hats and Children's Literature*. [Online.] Available at: www. villagehatshop.com/content/332/hats-and-childrens-literature.html (accessed: 12 June 2015).

Walliams, D. (2013) *Gangsta Granny*. London: HarperCollins Children's Books.

Warber, A. (2014) How to create your own mythological creature. *eHow*, 17 April. [Online.] Available at: www.ehow.com/how_4489533_create-own-mythological-creature.html (accessed: 25 May 2014).

Ward, V. (2013) Black characters put parents off books, new Children's Laureate says. *The Telegraph*, 4 June. [Online.] Available at: www.telegraph.co.uk/culture/books/10098595/Black-characters-put-parents-off-books-new-Childrens-Laureate-says.html (accessed: 30 November 2014).

Wenner, M. (2009) The serious need for play. *Scientific American Mind*, February. [Online.] Available at: www.scientificamerican.com/article.cfm?id=the-serious-need-for-play (accessed: 26 September 2013).

Whitaker, C. (n.d.) *Best Practices in Teaching Writing*. [Online.] Available at: www.learner. org/workshops/middlewriting/images/pdf/HomeBestPrac.pdf (accessed: 14 October 2014).

White, E.B. (2003) *Charlotte's Web*. London: Puffin.

Wilcox, A. (2013) *Descriptosaurus: Supporting Creative Writing for Ages 8–14*. Abingdon: Routledge.

Williams, C. (2008) *Mosaic*. [Online.] Available at: http://mosaicstory.com/ (accessed: 26 July 2014).

Williams, N.R. (2011) *Rescue Plot*. March 14. [Online.] Available at: http://nrwilliams. blogspot.co.uk/2011/03/rescue-plot.html (accessed: 25 September 2013).

Wilson, F. (1980) *Super Gran*. London: Puffin.

Wilson, G. (2013) *Breaking Through Barriers to Boys' Achievement*. 2nd edition. London: Bloomsbury Education.

Wilson, J. (2006) *The Suitcase Kid*. London: Corgi Yearling Books.

Wilson, J. (2008) *Midnight*. London: Corgi Yearling Books.

Winter, J.K. and Winter, E.J. (2009) *A Study of the Effect of Paper Color on Test Performance in Business Communication*. [Online.] Available at: http://rwahlers.iweb.bsu.edu/abd2009/Papers/p09_winter_winter.pdf (accessed: 19 May 2014).

Wright, A. (1997) *Creating Stories With Children*. Oxford: Oxford University Press.

Zike, D. (2008) *Dinah Zike's Foldables*. New York: Macmillan/McGraw-Hill.

Index